The Life and Work of W. Montgomery Watt

The Life and Work of W. Montgomery Watt

Edited by Carole Hillenbrand

EDINBURGH
University Press

Edinburgh University Press is one of the leading university presses in the UK. We publish academic books and journals in our selected subject areas across the humanities and social sciences, combining cutting-edge scholarship with high editorial and production values to produce academic works of lasting importance. For more information visit our website: edinburghuniversitypress.com

© editorial matter and organisation Carole Hillenbrand, 2019, 2020
© the chapters their several authors, 2019, 2020

Edinburgh University Press Ltd
The Tun – Holyrood Road
12 (2f) Jackson's Entry
Edinburgh EH8 8PJ

First published in hardback by Edinburgh University Press 2019

Typeset in 11/15 Adobe Garamond by
Servis Filmsetting Ltd, Stockport, Cheshire

A CIP record for this book is available from the British Library

ISBN 978 1 4744 4732 4 (hardback)
ISBN 978 1 4744 4733 1 (paperback)
ISBN 978 1 4744 4734 8 (webready PDF)
ISBN 978 1 4744 4735 5 (epub)

The right of the contributors to be identified as authors of this work has been asserted in accordance with the Copyright, Designs and Patents Act 1988 and the Copyright and Related Rights Regulations 2003 (SI No. 2498).

Published with the support of the University of Edinburgh Scholarly Publishing Initiatives Fund.

Frontispiece image © Ian Rhind

Contents

Preface vii

PART 1 Lectures Given on 23 October 2015 at the University of Edinburgh

1 William Montgomery Watt: the Man and the Scholar (Carole Hillenbrand) 3
2 The Study of Islam's Origins since William Montgomery Watt's Publications (Fred Donner) 19
3 Committed Openness: a Glance at William Montgomery Watt's Religious Life (Richard Holloway) 48

PART 2 Unpublished Writings of William Montgomery Watt

4 A Diary 55
5 'The Testament of a Search' and Later Unpublished Writings 67
6 William Montgomery Watt's Inaugural Lecture – Islamic Studies in Scotland: Retrospect and Prospect 87

PART 3 Reflections on the Work of William Montgomery Watt

7   Scottish Pioneers of Arabic and Islamic Studies: Reflections on Selected Parts of the Inaugural Lecture of Professor Watt, Given in Edinburgh in October 1965 (David Kerr)   107

APPENDICES

Appendix A: Some Reminiscences of Louis Massignon (William Montgomery Watt)   135

Appendix B: A Tribute to Professor Watt (Josef van Ess)   138

Appendix C: 'The Last Orientalist': a Valedictory Interview with Professor Watt (Bashir Maan and Alistair McIntosh)   146

Appendix D: A Tribute to Professor Watt (Hakim Mohammed Said)   156

Appendix E: William Montgomery Watt and a Historicist Interpretation of Islamic History (Hasan Hüseyin Adalıoğlu)   157

Appendix F: Obituaries of Professor Watt   159
  i.   Professor Hugh Goddard, University of Edinburgh, *The Scotsman*   159
  ii. Richard Holloway, Bishop of Edinburgh, *The Guardian*   163
  iii. Professor Carole Hillenbrand, *The Independent*   165
  iv. Ms Charlotte Alfred, a student of Islam at the University of Edinburgh in 2006, *Edinburgh Middle East Report Online*   168

A Bibliography of the Books Published by William Montgomery Watt   173
Index   176

Preface

The genesis of this book lies in a celebration of the fiftieth anniversary of the Inaugural Lecture of William Montgomery Watt as the first Professor of Arabic and Islamic Studies in Scotland in October 1965. This was held at the University of Edinburgh on Friday, 23 October 2015 in the august surroundings of the Playfair Library, and was entitled 'Islamic Studies in Scotland: Retrospect and Prospect'.

Professor Watt was based at the University of Edinburgh's Department of Arabic, which he led until his retirement in 1979, and over the years he became a towering global figure in the scholarly field of Islamic studies. Yet much has of course changed since Professor Watt's day, and this special event therefore sought both to look back on his contribution to his chosen field and also to assess scholarly developments in Islamic studies since his own seminal publications.

Professor Carole Hillenbrand, Professor Fred Donner and Bishop Richard Holloway were invited by the Department of Islamic and Middle Eastern Studies and the organisation now known as the Alwaleed Centre for the Study of Islam in the Contemporary World to deliver public lectures on Professor Watt as a man and as a scholar, on his religious life and on the development of Islamic studies over the past half-century. The event was introduced by the Senior Vice-Principal of the University of Edinburgh, Professor Charles Jeffery, and by the Head of the Department of Islamic and Middle Eastern Studies at the University of Edinburgh, Dr Tony Gorman. The following day, 24 October, the Playfair Library was again the venue for an international colloquium convened by Dr Andrew Marsham under the title 'Representations of Muhammad'. The following speakers took part: Dr Andreas Goerke, Professor Christiane Gruber, Professor Wilferd Madelung, Dr Nacim Pak-Shiraz, Dr Nicolai Sinai and Dr John Tolan. This event served to assess both the state of the field since Professor Watt's pioneering work and the latest scholarship on the subject. It also underlined the continuing importance of Islamic studies at the University of Edinburgh.

In the immediate aftermath of both these events two significant steps were taken. Firstly, as the former Head of the Department of Islamic and Middle Eastern Studies, I volunteered to edit a book about Professor Watt that would include contributions by those who spoke on 23 October as well as other relevant material. This book is the result of that decision. Secondly, the Department of Islamic and Middle Eastern Studies resolved to establish an annual lecture, named after Professor Watt, to be held at the University of Edinburgh.

It may be helpful to draw attention to a couple of technical matters here. Following the standard practice at Edinburgh University Press, transliteration of Arabic words has been kept to a minimum. The notes also follow the usual house style of The Press. I have occasionally added extra notes in some of the chapters, usually to give bibliographical details. In the citation of Professor Watt's book titles, only the place and date of publication are given in the notes. But in the bibliography of Professor Watt's books, given at the end of this volume, full details of the publisher are given.

There remains the pleasant duty of thanking all those who in their various ways helped to make this volume possible. Since it all began with the event launched to celebrate Professor Watt's contribution to Islamic studies both in Scotland and beyond, let me begin with those who had the idea and who made it a reality: my colleagues Dr Tony Gorman, whose brainchild it was; Dr Andrew Marsham, who oversaw the arrangements; and Professor Hugh Goddard, who helped to fund it by bringing it under the wing of the Alwaleed Centre. Dr Marsham also took on the onerous task of organising the day-long symposium that followed the celebration. I owe a great debt of gratitude to Professor Fred Donner and Bishop Richard Holloway for graciously agreeing to speak at the celebration. It was a pleasure to welcome all Professor Watt's children to that event, and I am especially glad to have had the valuable advice and help of Ann Watt during the course of editing this book. Dr Bashir Maan and Alastair Macintosh kindly agreed to the publication of their invaluable interview with Professor Watt in this book. My old friend Gun Kerr gave me an unpublished manuscript written by her late husband, Professor David Kerr, who held the post of Director of the Centre for the Study of Christianity in the Non-Western World at the University of Edinburgh until 2005, and I am delighted to be able to include that text here as a tribute to the memory of a dear friend and fellow-scholar. Finally, a big thank you to the team at Edinburgh University Press – Nicky Ramsey, Eddie Clark and other colleagues, including the copy-editor, Lel Gillingwater – who, as so often before, have generously placed their expertise at the disposal of this project and supported it unstintingly. I am certain that Professor Watt, who enjoyed a wonderfully productive relationship of many decades with Edinburgh University Press, would have wanted no other press to publish this book in memory of him.

Carole Hillenbrand

PART I

LECTURES GIVEN ON 23 OCTOBER 2015 AT THE UNIVERSITY OF EDINBURGH

1

William Montgomery Watt: the Man and the Scholar[1]

Carole Hillenbrand

Introduction

Professor William Montgomery Watt was a remarkable figure in the field of Islamic Studies who spent almost all his long career at the University of Edinburgh. As the first Professor of Arabic and Islamic Studies there, he gave his inaugural lecture, entitled 'Islamic Studies in Scotland: Retrospect and Prospect', on 21 October 1965. In his long lifetime, Professor Watt was probably the foremost Western non-Muslim interpreter of Islam, and he was a much-revered name for many Muslims all over the world. He died, aged ninety-seven, on 24 October 2006. Those who have worked or continue to work as scholars of Islamic and Middle Eastern studies at the University of Edinburgh – and they are an increasing number – have not forgotten his considerable achievements.

This chapter will be in two parts: firstly, it will give some insights into Professor Watt as a person, and secondly it will discuss his scholarly career. The information and reflections about him provided here have drawn on his published writings, on personal recollections of him gathered over a period spanning more than thirty years, and on the contents of an unpublished book of his, partly a kind of 'autobiography', called 'The Testament of a Search'.[2]

An Account of Professor Watt's Life [3]

William Montgomery Watt was born in 1909 in a small village in Fife called Ceres. His father, who was the Church of Scotland minister there, died when William was only fourteen months old, leaving his mother, aged thirty-nine, a widow and him an only child. They moved to Edinburgh where there were other family members. In 1919 William went to George Watson's College. There his headmaster persuaded him to study Classics, on the grounds that when he applied for a university place there would be more available scholarships in this subject for impecunious applicants. William reluctantly agreed; he writes in his unpublished autobiography:

> I thus became reconciled to the plan of studying Latin and Greek for the next five or six years, though I had no intention of devoting the rest of my life to this field. Already I was trying to work out ways of switching from Classics to philosophy.

He therefore studied for a four-year Classics degree at the University of Edinburgh, finishing it in 1929 in only three years. He then found enough financial support to go to Balliol College, Oxford, where he eagerly embarked on another undergraduate degree, specialising in philosophy and ancient history, followed by a BLitt on Emmanuel Kant. By then William had had enough of Oxford. Writing with a rare and disarming frankness in his autobiography, he says that through the Church he had made some good English friends: 'But I must be honest and state that on the whole I dislike the English.'

So he came back to Edinburgh in 1933 and began a PhD on what he describes vaguely as a topic in religion and science. A year later he started doing some undergraduate teaching to help out the Professor of Moral Philosophy.

The year 1937 proved to be a major turning point for William in a number of deeply significant ways. His mother died and shortly thereafter he left the Church of Scotland and joined the Episcopalian Church, which, as he wrote later, gave him the 'spiritual nurture' he needed to deal with his problems. His bereavement was followed by two other pivotal events: as he puts it quite frankly, 'my PhD was rejected without a chance of revising it', and he also published his first book, a vigorous critique of pacifism, called *Can Christians be Pacifists?*

Also in this year which proved so momentous for him, he met and befriended K. A. Mannan, a veterinary student from what later became Pakistan; William describes him as a 'keen and argumentative Muslim of the Ahmadiyya sect'. He took this young man in as a lodger and had lengthy conversations with him about Islam. It should also be noted that later on Mannan became a Sunni Muslim.

In 1938 William went south again; he studied at Cuddesdon Theological College outside Oxford and was ordained in the Episcopalian Church a year later. Back in Edinburgh he then served as curate of Old St Paul's Church for two years, and began a serious study of Arabic with Richard Bell, an original but still undervalued Qur'anic scholar, who was teaching Islamic studies at Edinburgh. William then started a PhD on a subject well suited to his interests and abilities, 'Predestination and Free Will in Islam'. In 1943 he married Jean Donaldson and finished his PhD.

An important new stage of his life then began. In January 1944 he went to Jerusalem as chaplain to the Anglican bishop. He was still there when Jewish terrorists blew up the King David Hotel in

1946. But he was afraid to stay there after that. In his autobiography, he writes that he had found Jerusalem disappointing because he had not had proper contact and discussion with Arab Muslim scholars. But he never forgot his sojourn in the Holy Land.

Soon after he returned to Scotland, on the retirement of his mentor Richard Bell, and he was appointed Lecturer in Arabic at the University of Edinburgh. That was in 1947 and here he was to spend nearly all his long and fruitful career. He was awarded a personal chair in 1964 and he retired from his post at the university in 1979. But he did not stop there. Indeed, for the majority of the remaining twenty-seven years of his life he kept doing what he liked doing most – writing books and articles.

Professor Watt was given a number of academic honours; he lectured briefly at the University of Toronto, the Collège de France and Georgetown University. He was awarded an honorary doctorate by the University of Aberdeen, received the prestigious American Giorgio Levi Della Vida Medal and was an early recipient of the British Society for Middle Eastern Studies award for services to the field.

Professor Watt kept his family matters private, but it was always clear that Jean was an ideal wife for him; she was warm, friendly and sociable, and the mainstay of family stability for him and their five children; one son and four daughters. He makes a rare reference to his family in the preface to one of his early and little-known books, *The Truth in the Religions; a Sociological and Psychological Approach*.[4] There he writes: 'As for my wife and family, I can only speak with the highest praise of the good humour and resilience with which they endured my vagaries and eccentricities during the six months when the book was actually being written.'

Later, in the first draft of his unpublished autobiography completed around 1974, he says that the secure base in his home has been an important factor in all that he has achieved. He had a cosy house, appropriately called the Neuk, in Dalkeith, a village outside Edinburgh, and every summer the Watt family used to decamp to their second house, beautifully situated by the sea in Fife.

Outside the family Professor Watt was a shy, withdrawn person, not easy to chat with. Indeed, he had no small talk at all. A conversation with him soon moved to weighty religious matters and it stayed there. He was lofty and remote, even Olympian, in manner. There was always a sense of distance. His expression, however, was always kindly and unthreatening and I never found him to be malicious about anyone. One reference in his unpublished autobiography is revealing in this respect; there he writes: 'I sometimes shrink from meeting other people in a friendly open way because I am afraid of some sort of rejection.' Being the only child of a lonely young widow and spending most of his childhood with adults must have contributed to his introspective and inhibited social manner.

In his autobiography he is disarmingly frank about his first years at the University of Edinburgh as a lecturer in Arabic and Islamic studies. He writes that he had to produce a four-year honours course in Arabic, without ever having been through such a course himself as a student. He remarks that fortunately, in his first year of teaching Arabic, there were no students in the third and fourth years of the course, and to quote his own words: 'I was broken in gradually (and) my Arabic improved somewhat.'

By the 1970s Professor Watt was well launched into building up Islamic studies at Edinburgh, not through increasing the undergraduate intake, which was small, but by agreeing to supervise large numbers of doctoral students from the Arab world and Pakistan. These students were drawn to Edinburgh because of his stellar publishing reputation. Although he had a famously light touch, perhaps seeing them once a term, they were very happy to say that they were working under his supervision.

Professor Watt's reputation lingered on long after his retirement. Indeed, it was because of him that the University of Baghdad chose the University of Edinburgh as the best place in the UK in which to endow a new Iraq Chair of Arabic and Islamic Studies.

When I travelled to the Middle East, Pakistan and Malaysia in the 1980s and 1990s, to attend conferences or give lectures, it would be true to say that I found the reputation of Professor Watt to be nothing short of legendary in these countries. I was frequently asked: 'Do you know Professor Watt?' After I had said yes, many doors were opened for me and I was bathed, as it were, in his aura. All the Muslim academics I met praised him to the skies for what he had done for Islamic studies.

What happened after his official retirement? Quite simply, as I have already said, he went on writing.[5] So for the next twenty years or more I would, at his request, visit him regularly for coffee in his home several times a term. We would then talk for an hour or two. During my many visits there he would talk about his publications, his future projects and, most of all, his ideas on many aspects of religion. He did not gossip or reminisce.

He rarely came in to the University of Edinburgh; indeed, I met him only once in the department when he attended an afternoon seminar. He appeared to be fast asleep throughout the event but when the speaker's talk ended he was the first to ask him a question, and a very penetrating question it was. However, in his study at home in the mornings when I visited him he was always very alert right through his seventies and eighties.

I spent a number of memorable moments with him. One such occasion was a visit of the eminent German scholar of Islamic studies, Professor Annemarie Schimmel, who held chairs simultaneously at Harvard and Bonn. That was the only time that Professor Watt visited our house in Edinburgh. On the matter of malt whisky, the national drink of his homeland, he was a true Scotsman. We watched incredulously as he and Professor Schimmel had a really great time; her full-blown eccentric and warm personality broke down his usually shy manner. They were both very relaxed, ever more so, as they gradually enjoyed generous quantities of malt whisky without any outside help during the evening.

My husband Robert and I gave him a bottle of malt whisky for his ninetieth birthday present and we attended his party. He wrote us a charming letter of thanks which I have kept. Speaking of the whisky he said in the letter: 'Though my sense of taste is now somewhat impaired I get a good flavour from it and am thoroughly enjoying it.' Thus, William's life was not always full of grim tussles with metaphysical issues.

One day in the late 1990s he suddenly said to me: 'I have been thinking that I would like to give my personal library to Edinburgh University. Would you please be my executor and organise this for me?' This was a marvellous surprise. And indeed more than 900 volumes of his were donated to the University of Edinburgh Library soon afterwards and they are housed there as *The Watt Collection*.

Professor Watt, the Scholar

Over the last forty years, and indeed until the present turmoil began, most scholars specialising in Arabic and Islam have been eager to visit Muslim-majority countries and to live there for extended periods. Not so with Professor Watt and many of his European contemporaries. Such men were, to use the German term, *Stubengelehrten*, 'armchair scholars'. Apart from a few visits to occasional conferences, they kept at a safe distance from the Middle East, South Asia and beyond. That led to an overriding emphasis on texts rather than on other roads to knowledge, such as personal experience, residence in Islamic countries, fieldwork and discussions with Muslims on the spot. Inevitably, therefore, this resulted in a somewhat rarefied, intellectualised approach.

In the field of Islamic studies, Professor Watt's output was colossal, ranging from popular introductory books to scholarly monographs. He published a phenomenal thirty-three books and literally hundreds of articles and book reviews. Of the books, twenty-one are about aspects of Islam and the Muslim world,[6] one is a translation from Arabic of parts of a treatise called *The Book of Demonstration* (written by Eutychius, a tenth-century Bishop of Alexandria)[7] and his other books are about Christianity and religion more generally. He was very pleased that a good number of his books had been translated into other languages.

In 1948 he published his first book on Islam; it was his PhD thesis, entitled *Free Will and Predestination in Early Islam*.[8] This heralded the beginning of one of his abiding academic preoccupations – the study of Islamic theology.

Early in his career he focused especially on the career of the Prophet Muhammad. For these writings he made a close analysis of the original Arabic sources; the result was two classics, *Muhammad at Mecca*[9] and *Muhammad at Medina*.[10] The second of these is a particularly impressive work on Muhammad, as the founder of the first Muslim community, the *umma*, and as a lawmaker. In 1961 Professor Watt wrote a third, shorter book which condensed the previous two, *Muhammad: Prophet and Statesman*.[11] It is these three books on Muhammad that have made him so famous in Muslim-majority countries. He was always aware of what Muslims might think and how they would feel when non-Muslims write about Islam and their Prophet. Of course, since his first publications on Muhammad, much new research has been published by later scholars who were not as scrupulously concerned as Professor Watt was about whether Muslims approved or disapproved of what they wrote. These later scholars have excavated the historical origins of Islam, also using non-Islamic sources, rather than accepting the salvation history of the new faith that developed in Muslim lands after the death of Muhammad.

Professor Watt saw part of his brief as setting out to correct the deep-rooted negative images of Islam and Muhammad that had prevailed in Europe since the Crusading period. In his book *Muhammad: Prophet and Statesman*, he emphasises the Abrahamic foundation of Islam and its links with Judaism and Christianity. He writes: 'Islam is "a form of the religion of Abraham" – a form, too, well suited to the outlook of men whose way of life was closer to Abraham than that of the bulk of Jews and Christians.'[12] Later, in his handwritten autobiography, he sums up his lifelong approach to Muhammad as follows: 'From an early date I held that Muhammad must have been sincere. It is unthinkable that a great world religion should have been based on imposture or falsehood.'

However, Professor Watt was not always afraid to experiment with new schools of thought and methodology. Quite early in his academic career, in 1961, he published a book called *Islam and the Integration of Society*.[13] In this work, influenced by Max Weber, he uses sociology and economic history to interpret the beginnings of Islam. But the book had little impact; as the great German scholar of Islam, Josef van Ess, said: 'The book remained a call in the wilderness; there was not much discussion of it and almost no attempt to carry it forward.'[14] And in any case Professor Watt did not follow up this approach.

For my personal taste his most impressive book is *The Formative Period of Islamic Thought*.[15] This outlines with admirable lucidity the major developments in Islamic theology from the death of Muhammad until around the year 950. Continuing in this line of enquiry, he also published *The Faith and Practice of al-Ghazali*,[16] a translation of the spiritual 'autobiography' of the great medieval Muslim scholar, al-Ghazali (d. 1111), written in Arabic and entitled *Al-munqidh min al-dalal (The Deliverer from Error)*, and he followed that with an excellent study of al-Ghazali entitled *Muslim Intellectual: a Study of al-Ghazali*.[17]

At the time of Professor Watt's death in 2006, Timothy Wright, the Chief Executive of Edinburgh University Press (EUP), wrote the following words to Jean Watt, his widow:

> It goes without saying that Professor Watt was an enormously important figure in the history of the Press, establishing as he did in 1962 the *Islamic Surveys* series and spending twenty years as its editor. The series is still one of the most successful that the Press has and it laid the foundation for what is now widely regarded as one of the leading Islamic lists in the country.[18]

Professor Watt's achievements with the highly successful EUP *Islamic Surveys* series were twofold. Firstly, serving as commissioning editor from 1962 until 1980, he masterminded the setting up and continuing regular output of handbooks intended for students and the general reader. He judged this rightly as an important aspect of an academic's work. And secondly, he practised what he preached. He showed the way by writing seven books of his own in this series, which proved to be very popular and useful in the classroom. He had a way of writing which simplified and clarified complex topics. Inevitably, in all these seven books, he was not equally sure-footed. He was less at ease with historical subjects, such as *A History of Islamic Spain*,[19] or *The Influence of Islam on Medieval Europe*,[20] where he mostly summarised the work of other scholars. On the other hand, he was on his home territory when writing the other four books in this series, which were fine short overviews of Islamic thought – entitled *Islamic Philosophy and Theology*,[21] *Islamic Political Thought*[22] and *Islamic Creeds*.[23] Professor Watt's EUP books have sold phenomenally well. According to Nicola Ramsey, Publisher for Islamic and Middle Eastern Studies at EUP, it is fair to say that, from the 1960s until now, at least

25,000–30,000 copies of Professor Watt's books have been sold – a truly wonderful achievement.

In similarly popular vein, but with other publishing houses, Professor Watt wrote short histories of Islam, and a book entitled *The Majesty That Was Islam*,[24] a cultural and social overview of the period 661–1100.

He also wrote books on non-Islamic subjects. From the very beginning of his career as an author he published short books about his own faith, Christianity. Two such works appeared in quick succession: *The Reality of God* (1957)[25] and *The Cure for Human Troubles: a Statement of the Christian Message in Modern Times* (1959).[26] These are evangelical tracts. In his autobiography he mentions rather ruefully that he has published books outside the field of Islamic studies 'though they have received much less attention than my books on strictly Islamic subjects'. This frank admission proves true especially for his writings on Christianity. These earned him very little praise and were indeed on occasion turned down later in his retirement by publishers, such as the Society for Promoting Christian Knowledge (SPCK), who had published some of his books in the past.

One late work, entitled *Islamic Fundamentalism and Modernity*,[27] was published in 1988; this concerned current issues to do with Islam in the modern world. It made little impact. Then, in 1991, he brought out the book *Muslim–Christian Encounters: Perceptions and Misperceptions*;[28] in it he covers the first contacts between Eastern Christians and Muslims in the seventh century and he brings his account right up until the Salman Rushdie affair. In his review of this book, the American Muslim scholar Mahmoud Ayoub, whilst saying that Professor Watt's discussion adds nothing new, describes it as engaging, lucid and fair throughout.[29] Right to the end, therefore, Professor Watt manages to clarify material that is little known to the reading public in the West. And as a final publication at the age of eighty-four he returns full circle to his early passion for philosophy in a book entitled *Religious Truth for Our Time*.[30] Here he examines grandiose topics such as the limitations of human thought and language, the nature of truth and the impact of the new global order.

Despite the wide range of topics covered in Professor Watt's vastly prolific writings, certain deeply entrenched views remained constant. Long before the recent wave of Islamophobia in the West, he advocated the necessity of dialogue with Muslims, not demonisation of them. He doubted the appropriateness of conversion and felt that those of all faiths should collaborate in friendship to stem the tide of materialism and secularisation. In my last few conversations with him he expressed opinions almost exclusively the same as those which he had held when I first met him; but now in his extreme old age they had become even more urgent for him. In particular, he mentioned how much he wished that Christians could accept the prophethood of Muhammad: long ago, in his book *Muhammad at Mecca* he had written the following: 'I consider that Muhammad was truly a prophet and I think that we Christians should admit this.'[31] He deeply regretted the fact that whilst Christians could share without difficulty the monotheism of the first line of the Muslim *shahada* (the profession of faith): 'I testify that there is no god but God', they were unable to accept the second half of the *shahada*: 'I testify that Muhammad is the Messenger of God.'

Moreover, Professor Watt often mentioned that the Islamic emphasis on the uncompromising oneness of God had caused him to reconsider the Christian doctrine of the Trinity, a doctrine which is vigorously attacked in the Qur'an as undermining true monotheism. Influenced by Islam, with its ninety-nine names of God, each expressing a special attribute of God, Professor Watt returned to the Latin word 'persona' – which meant a 'face' or 'mask', and not 'individual', as it now means in English – and he formulated the view that a truer interpretation of the Christian Trinity would not signify that God comprises three entities. For him, the Trinity represents three different 'faces' of the one and the same God.[32]

After his retirement in 1979, throughout the 1980s and 1990s, when increasing pressure was beginning to be placed on non-publishing academics, forcing them to produce at least a modest body of research to justify their status as scholars, Professor Watt was busy writing at home in retirement, far away from such pressures. He was never afraid of hard work, and he worked as hard in retirement as he had whilst in post. The truth is that he was totally committed to research and publication and he made that his priority for the entire time that he worked as a scholar of Islam in Edinburgh, both when he was in post and also in his long retirement. Students, whether undergraduates or graduates, were of secondary interest in comparison. But the sheer number of Muslim postgraduates who came to Edinburgh to study with him year-on-year changed the very face of the department.

It is appropriate now to write a little more about Professor Watt's unpublished autobiography. As already mentioned, in the late 1990s he gave me a copy of this work and he asked me to try to find a publisher for it. He had apparently tried and failed to do so. I too had no success in this. The fact of the matter appeared to be that he was a highly successful and prolific world-famous scholar of Islam; but he also always wanted to be recognised in matters Christian. And this recognition was simply never accorded to him. So this personal memoir of his, which is not exactly a traditional autobiography but is more an account of his long spiritual and intellectual journey in search of religious truth, has remained unpublished. Much of its contents, such as chapters on religion and science and his encounter with sociology and psychology, are very outdated now. But the document contains a good number of very interesting insights into his personal development and his thinking about Islam and Muslim–Christian relations. The work is in two parts. The first part was completed around 1974 and contains valuable autobiographical remarks. The second part, written at a later stage, is philosophical in tone and is almost entirely about his views on Christianity; indeed, he wished this part to be exemplary rather than personal: 'I have deliberately kept the autobiographical element to a minimum, since I felt that much of what I was saying was not just my own ideas, but had a measure of objective truth.' In a sense I have always felt that in this work he wanted to chart the stages in his own spiritual development in a way similar to that adopted by al-Ghazali or perhaps even St Augustine.

In his advanced old age, Professor Watt still cared about the Israel–Palestine issue and he said that he had become increasingly convinced that there can be no lasting solution to the Palestine problem which does not bring in all three religions for which Jerusalem is sacred. And to the last he had not forgotten his two-year stay in Jerusalem. It was therefore revealing that the church collection at his funeral in 2006 was given to Medical Aid for Palestinians. Above all, Professor Watt wanted a rapprochement between Christians and Muslims; indeed, at his funeral service, as well as two readings from the Bible, part of Chapter 6 of the Qur'an was read out in English translation.

Professor Watt believed in dialogue, in which he himself had long played the role of facilitator, a twofold dialogue held on the one hand between him and his own non-Muslim society in order to promote understanding of Islam and Muslims, and on the other hand an interfaith dialogue between Christians and Muslims. In his discussions he was not polemical. Van Ess describes him as 'intellectually detached from both religions, while continuing to practise one'.[33] Professor Watt himself writes: 'While adhering to scholarly standards I have been as sympathetic as possible to Islam.' This approach is apparent above all in his writings about Muhammad.

In his autobiography Professor Watt speaks of a reality underlying religious experience. Whilst there is no exact way of translating a Christian doctrine into Islamic terms and vice versa, he writes: 'I am convinced that the same reality underlies the experience of both religions.' Time alone will tell whether this insight proves prophetic. But for now, it is clear that in the present climate of Islamophobia across many parts of the world, Professor Watt's inspiring writings still have much to teach us.

Notes

1. This chapter is a slightly revised version of my lecture given at the Edinburgh conference in October 2015. The text of the lecture can be found at: 'Lecture by Professor Carole Hillenbrand in event: Islamic Studies in Scotland: Retrospect and Prospect', University of Edinburgh, Islamic and Middle Eastern Studies, available at <https://www.ed.ac.uk/files/atoms/files/professor_carole_hillenbrand.pdf> (last accessed 28 April 2018).
2. Professor Watt gave me a handwritten copy of this diary in the 1990s. He was keen for it to be published eventually.
3. Professor William Montgomery Watt will be referred to in this book as either William or as Professor Watt, depending on the context.
4. Edinburgh, 1963, v.
5. It was in this period of his life that I got to know him. I had seen him in passing when I was a postgraduate in Edinburgh, but I never actually worked with him, because I joined the academic staff of Islamic and Middle Eastern Studies as a junior lecturer in 1979 just after he had retired. But he chaired the committee that appointed me.
6. For full details, see the bibliography at the end of this book.
7. Eutychius, *The Book of Demonstration*, 2 vols, trans. W. Montgomery Watt, Louvain, 1960.
8. London, 1948.

9. Oxford, 1953.
10. Oxford, 1956.
11. Oxford, 1961.
12. *Muhammad: Prophet and Statesman*, 118.
13. London, 1961.
14. Josef van Ess, 'Tribute to Professor Watt', in *Islam: Past Influence and Present Challenge*, eds Alford T. Welch and Pierre Cachia, Edinburgh, 1979, ix–xiv.
15. Edinburgh, 1973.
16. *The Faith and Practice of al-Ghazali*, London, 1953.
17. Edinburgh, 1963.
18. Quoted from a copy of a personal letter from Timothy Wright.
19. Co-authored with Pierre Cachia, Edinburgh, 1965.
20. Edinburgh, 1972.
21. Edinburgh, 1962.
22. Edinburgh, 1968.
23. Edinburgh, 1994.
24. London, 1974.
25. London, 1957.
26. London, 1959.
27. London and New York, 1988.
28. London, 1991.
29. Mahmoud Ayoub, 'Review of William Montgomery Watt, Muslim–Christian Encounters: Perceptions and Misperceptions, London, 1991', *International Journal of Middle East Studies*, November 2003; available at: <https://doi.org/10.1017/S0020743800059493> (last accessed 28 April 2018).
30. London, 1995.
31. *Muhammad at Mecca*, 1.
32. This theme is discussed in his unpublished autobiography.
33. Van Ess, 'Tribute', xiii.

2

The Study of Islam's Origins since William Montgomery Watt's Publications

Fred Donner

William Montgomery Watt (1909–2006) was one of the most important and respected scholars of Islamic studies alive when I was beginning my scholarly career in the late 1960s and early 1970s – certainly, he was one of the most important for me, although, unfortunately, I never had the opportunity to meet him in person. His numerous studies – above all his works on the Prophet Muhammad[1] and his several short introductory volumes in the Edinburgh University Press's *Islamic Surveys* series (which he instigated), especially his *Islamic Philosophy and Theology* (1962) and *Islamic Political Thought: the Basic Concepts* (1968) – were, on the one hand, models of lucid, careful scholarship and, on the other, incredibly helpful introductions to various topics within Islamic studies. Without his work to learn from and absorb, I know that my own development as a scholar would have been far more difficult, and much less pleasant. And I am sure that I am not the only scholar of my generation who owes such a debt to Professor Watt and his work.

Watt's Work in its Time

Reflecting back on his work forty years later, however, it is possible to see it with more perspective. I still esteem it very highly, but now I can also see Watt's contributions as products of their time. The social sciences, after a period of gestation in the first half of the twentieth century, became in the years following World War II the regnant academic disciplines in much of the Western academy (and outside it, in the arena of policy formation). Watt's work, like that of everyone else in that time, reflects this. His interpretation of Muhammad's life, for example, focuses on the economic and social tensions that, he argued, had developed in Meccan society because of the nascent inequality produced by the burgeoning commerce of Mecca. He spoke of the demise – under the corrosive effect of the growing rift between rich and poor – of what he called 'tribal humanism', the ethos of mutual responsibility according to which members of a tribe shared and looked after each other. Watt saw Muhammad's teachings as, in part, a response to this essentially socio-economic and, hence, moral dislocation in Meccan society. There was relatively little emphasis on the impact of Muhammad's religious ideas as a factor in Islam's appearance.

Watt's work on Muhammad resembled in some respects the earlier work of Hubert Grimme (1864–1942). Grimme had argued that Muhammad was not a religious preacher, but a social reformer, concerned with succouring orphans and widows, and the poor generally.[2] This view was, however, almost immediately criticised by other scholars, who emphasised the centrality in Muhammad's teachings of the idea of God's oneness and concern with the Last Judgement and the afterlife, concerns that went far beyond merely mundane social issues.

Watt did not deny Muhammad's religious role – far from it; indeed, he seems to have accepted that Muhammad had been sincere in presenting himself as a prophet, and always spoke of Muhammad in a tone of respect that bordered on reverence. But he did not expend much ink on elaborating how Muhammad's religious message contributed to the success of the movement he had begun, nor did he explore very deeply how Muhammad's religious message fit into currents of religious thought in the seventh-century Near East. This tepid engagement by Watt with the religious aspects of Muhammad's mission was also in keeping with the outlook of the social sciences of his day. Social scientists at that time, and secular-minded historians above all, were uncomfortable talking about religion, and had particular difficulty accepting religion as a factor of historical explanation. So they often engaged in a kind of reductionism when speaking of early Islam, explaining away Islam's worldly success as being due to something else, searching for what they considered the 'real cause' – anything other than religion: the desiccation of Arabia, the lust for booty among Arabian tribesmen, the desire to open new commercial markets, the expression of a presumed 'Arab' national feeling, the exhaustion of the two great empires, the social integration brought by Islam that unleashed the latent energy of a hitherto fragmented tribal society (this last one being my own contribution to the reductionist agenda).[3] Watt was swimming in these secular waters too; the secular tone of his work was pronounced enough that the French Islamicist Georges-Henri Bousquet (1900–78) gave his review of Watt's *Muhammad at Mecca* the wonderfully ironic title 'A Marxist interpretation of the origins of Islam by an Episcopal clergyman'.[4]

Watt's work also represented an earlier phase of scholarship in its assumptions about the sources for Islam's beginnings. Watt took a fairly sanguine view of the traditional Islamic narrative sources – the chronicles, biographical dictionaries, works of genealogy, collections of poetry and belletristic prose, works of theology, and even the collections of *hadith* or sayings attributed to the

Prophet Muhammad – that provided almost all the evidence for his reconstruction of the events of Muhammad's life and Islam's origins. In accepting the general reliability of these sources, Watt was doing what almost everyone else did prior to the 1970s. A few scholars had raised questions about the reliability of the traditional Islamic sources – notably the Hungarian scholar Ignác Goldziher (1850–1921), the Belgian Henri Lammens (1862–1937) and the German Josef Schacht (1902–69). But their trenchant criticisms of Islamic tradition were either brushed aside by most scholars, or said to apply only to legal injunctions and not to be relevant to the historical sources that described the events and personalities associated with the rise of Islam.

The Study of Islamic Origins since Watt's Heyday

How, then, have studies of early Islam changed since Watt's day? It is perhaps a little misleading, actually, to speak in this way, because Watt's day is hardly over – he continued to publish until a few years before his death in 2006; the last of his books appeared in 2002, when he was ninety-three. But we can say that the scholarly ground was changing rather dramatically under Watt's feet just about the time he retired from the University of Edinburgh in 1979.

The change had somewhat quiet roots, however noisy – as will be seen shortly – its later manifestations may have become. One of the first decisive contributions was the publication – if one can call it that – of the *Habilitationsschrift*, or second German dissertation of Albrecht Noth (1937–99), which had the intimidating title *Quellenkritische Untersuchungen zu Themen, Formen, und Tendenzen frühislamischer Geschichtsüberlieferung* (*Source-critical Investigations into Themes, Forms, and Agendas of Early Islamic Historical Tradition*). This appeared in 1970, but because it was in German – and in a rather difficult German at that – and because it was not published by a regular academic publishing house but rather was cheaply produced in a softcover issued by the Oriental Seminar of the University of Bonn, where Noth was teaching, the book had limited circulation even within Germany and became only slowly known to other scholars. A second edition was subsequently produced, translated into English, by Lawrence I. Conrad, as *The Early Arabic Historical Tradition: a Source-critical Study*.[5] Noth's book, and some of his subsequent articles, challenged the factual reliability of the corpus of Islamic historical accounts about early Islam, especially about the conquests that followed closely after Muhammad's death, which Noth subjected for the first time to the kind of form-critical and text-critical analysis that had long been routine in studies of the Hebrew Bible and the Christian Gospels. This was not an accident; Albrecht's father, Martin Noth (1902–68), was one of the leading German scholars of the Old Testament in the middle years of the century, so the young Albrecht was probably served text-critical perspectives along with his breakfast cereal whilst growing up in the Noth household. The effect of Albrecht Noth's work was to cast doubt on the accuracy or truthfulness of the traditional Islamic origins narrative, but he did not yet offer any alternative view of those origins.

Another decisive contribution to this changing terrain in early Islamic studies was the appearance, in the 1970s, of revisionist works on the Qur'an text. Although Western scholars, as non-Muslims, did not consider the Qur'an to be God's word, as devout Muslims do, most Western scholars assumed that the Qur'an was essentially a product of Muhammad's own life and thought, and tried to understand it in the context of the standard Islamic biography of Muhammad's life, the *Sira* of Ibn Ishaq.[6] The first blow against this consensus view of the Qur'an also came from Germany, in the 1970 dissertation and subsequent book by Günter Lüling (1928–2014), *Über den Ur-Koran* (*On the Original Qur'an*).[7] For reasons of academic politics, which will not be detailed here, Lüling was driven out of the German university system and his work was subjected to a conspiracy of silence by the German academic establishment for several decades. He became an academic outcast, had to self-publish his several books and, because those books were written in German, they too became known only slowly to scholars elsewhere. Lüling's critique was theologically based and proposed an alternative view of how the Qur'an had developed and, consequently, of Muhammad's career. In Lüling's view, the Qur'an was in part a reworking of older liturgical hymns of a hitherto unknown Arabic-speaking Christian community in Mecca. According to him, Muhammad had begun his life as a member of this Christian cult, but came to disagree with some of its theology and consequently altered these strophic hymns to reflect his new religious views. Lüling attempted, by making various changes to the standard Qur'an text, to uncover what he thought was their original Christian meaning. Lüling's proposed emendations, as they gradually became known, were criticised by many as arbitrary and unfounded, and his ideas have not gained much support, but he did advance many perceptive insights on the Qur'an and was one of the first to challenge directly the inherited consensus views of the Qur'an and of Muhammad's life.

More serious for the scholarly establishment of Islamicists was the publication by John Wansbrough (1928–2002) of his book *Qur'anic Studies*, which was produced by Oxford University Press in 1977. The prestige of its imprimatur, Wansbrough's status as a respected professor at London's School of Oriental and African Studies (SOAS), and the fact that the book was in English meant that scholars everywhere quickly took notice of it (although its English style is often so dense that, for many readers, it might as well have been written in academic German). On the basis of a literary analysis of the Qur'an, Wansbrough proposed (among other things) that the text of the Qur'an was not mainly the product of

Muhammad's time, but rather a text that coalesced as a codified, closed canon of scripture only gradually, over a period of more than 200 years. He also suggested that the likely place of its origin was not Muhammad's Mecca, but the 'sectarian milieu' of inter-confessional religious debate somewhere in the Fertile Crescent, possibly southern Iraq. This work, too, implied that the traditional narrative about how Islam began was not just wrong, but was actually intentionally misleading, an exercise in the writing of *ex post facto* salvation history by the later community – a notion that was also embedded, if only implicitly, in Noth's study of the historiographical tradition.

As noted earlier, these works represent what we might call the quiet beginnings of the revisionist wave of works on early Islam that began in the 1970s: quiet in Noth's and Lüling's case because their works were in German and poorly disseminated, and in Wansbrough's case because of the forbidding difficulty of his prose (one colleague even suggested to me that someone should review Wansbrough's book, ending with the comment that it was important, and that a competent English translation was greatly to be desired).

The noisy phase of the wave of revisionist scholarship came first and foremost with the publication, also in 1977, of the book *Hagarism: the Making of the Islamic World* by Patricia Crone (1945–2015) and Michael Cook (1940–).[8] They built on the historiographical critique of Noth, the earlier sceptical opinions of scholars like Goldziher and Schacht, and were probably inspired in some way by the work of Wansbrough (who was their colleague at London's SOAS, but whose relationship to their work, if any, has remained unclear and unarticulated). On this basis, Crone and Cook fashioned a radically new reconstruction of early Islamic history. In doing so, they set aside almost completely the traditional Islamic sources as historiographically suspect and drew instead mainly on the testimony of seventh-century non-Muslim sources in Greek, Armenian, Syriac and other languages, as well as on some seventh-century documents. Theirs was not the first attempt to utilise the non-Muslim sources systematically to talk about Islam's beginnings (the Byzantinist Walter Kaegi may have been the pioneer in this regard)[9] but, unlike earlier scholars, Crone and Cook assembled from these sources a revisionist narrative that struck many people familiar with the traditional origins story as little short of scandalous. Relying on the seventh-century chronicle attributed to the Armenian bishop Sebeos, they proposed, among other things, that Islam began when Jews evicted by the Byzantines from Edessa fled to Arabia and joined forces with Muhammad's followers in order to reconquer the Holy Land, above all Jerusalem, from the Byzantines. Drawing on other sources, they argued that Muhammad was still alive when the conquests in Palestine began; that the original Muslim sanctuary was located somewhere in the northern Hijaz, not in Mecca, and that the story of Muhammad's career in Mecca was a later fiction; that the caliph Abu Bakr never existed, but was 'invented' when Muhammad's death was back-dated to fill the gap between his 'new' death date and the beginning of the reign of the second caliph, 'Umar – who, since he was called *al-faruq*, 'the redeemer', had to follow immediately upon the Prophet in any case. For Watt, who had spent his whole career elaborating aspects of a narrative of early Islam that closely followed the traditional paradigm, these ideas – appearing just two years before his retirement – must have been a kind of nightmare, as it was for many other established scholars. The rather sensational manner in which *Hagarism*'s claims were presented suggested that there could be no compromise between its new views and the traditional account; but the fact that *Hagarism* built its arguments on unimpeachable sources of evidence and for the most part used them quite judiciously made it impossible simply to dismiss its arguments out of hand as crank literature. What Crone and Cook did, essentially, was to pose a blunt challenge to historians of early Islam: are you going to behave as proper historians, and subject the sources you use to rigorous source criticism? Or are you going simply to look the other way when the limitations of the Islamic sources become apparent, and continue to preach their religiously grounded vision of the past?

All of these developments, but particularly the publication of *Hagarism*, with its provocative manner of presentation, ignited a firestorm of intense discussion among scholars (and some non-scholars)[10] about Islam's origins. (Watt himself responded to some of the revisionist critique, in characteristically measured fashion, in his 1988 book *Muhammad's Mecca: History in the Qur'an*).[11] The appearance of these first revisionist works completely revitalised the study of early Islam, which for some time had been a rather sleepy and unexciting field, and placed it on much more secure foundations. The electrifying realisation that there were fundamental historical questions still to be resolved drew in scores of new researchers, most of whom also approached the task with a keen awareness of the need to handle evidence in a manner that could withstand the most careful scrutiny. These early revisionist works, therefore, marked a real turning point in the history of our field, and it is for this reason that I consider *Hagarism* perhaps the most important single book in Islamic studies of the twentieth century.[12] It was important not because of its reconstruction of early Islamic history, many aspects of which are, I think, simply wrong, but because it led all of us to work with much greater methodological integrity and awareness. And, it inaugurated a veritable flood of subsequent researches, and set the agenda for the study of early Islam right up until the present, and with no end in sight.

There was another dimension to the sea change that came over early Islamic studies in the 1970s, one that was not directly related to the rise of source-critical studies and revisionist history in the style of *Hagarism* that we have just described. It had to do with the emergence of what we can broadly call 'Late Antiquity studies', which burst on the scene rather suddenly following the appearance of Peter Brown's epoch-making book *The World of Late Antiquity* in 1971.[13] Before its publication, one finds hardly any book titles that include the phrase 'Late Antiquity', except among German art historians, who occasionally referred to the art of the *Spätantike*. After 1971, however, scores of books (and hundreds of articles) making reference to Late Antiquity appear; and some of these works have relevance for our concerns, because Brown's book *The World of Late Antiquity* included a consideration of early Islamic history (to the fall of the Umayyads and early 'Abbasids) as a final chapter of Late Antiquity. In effect, what Brown did was to synthesise several fields of study that had hitherto been largely separate, pursued by discrete communities of scholars who did not talk much to one another: the field of late Roman (or early Byzantine) history, the field of church history, especially the history of the eastern churches (which had been a rather musty subject pursued mostly by scholars in religious orders), the study of Sasanian history (pursued by almost no one), and the study of early Islamic history. Brown conceived of Late Antiquity as extending from the second to the eighth centuries CE in the Near East and Mediterranean, and portrayed this period as one of dynamic cultural and social creativity rather than 'decline'.

Brown's integration of early Islamic history into the framework of Late Antiquity broadened the perspective of historians of early Islam, and we might consider the approach taken by Crone and Cook in *Hagarism* to be in part a kind of response to Brown's *World of Late Antiquity*, which had been published six years earlier; like it, *Hagarism* integrated evidence from Syriac and other non-Muslim source languages, and various kinds of documentary evidence. The rush of new work on early Islam that emerged in the

1980s and has continued unabated ever since reflects this broadened perspective. We see it not only in the increased attention paid to Syriac, Armenian, Coptic and other literary sources dating from the seventh century, but also in a renewed interest in various forms of documentary evidence for this period. Studies of the coins and seals of the early Islamic and of the Byzantine and Sasanian empires, formerly the province of a mere handful of scholars, proliferated rapidly in number and increased in sophistication, and became the primary occupation of a growing number of scholars, rather than merely a sideline pursued by historians whose main concerns were elsewhere. Whereas in the 1950s and 1960s 'Islamic numismatics' was more or less synonymous with the name of George Miles, by the 1990s scores of scholars were engaged.

A similar, if even more delayed, transformation occurred in the field of papyrology. The existence of papyri from the seventh century, written in Greek, Coptic and Arabic, had long been known, but they had not, with few exceptions, been much used by historians.[14] Moreover, aside from the indefatigable Adolf Grohmann (1887–1977),[15] few made the study of Arabic papyri, particularly those of the early Islamic period, the main focus of their research. It was not until the 1980s and especially the first decade of the twenty-first century that the number of scholars working actively in Arabic papyrology began to swell markedly (though not all focused on the earliest Islamic period).[16]

Even more striking were developments in the study of the archaeology of the early Islamic period. Until the 1960s relatively little archaeological work had been undertaken that focused on the Islamic period in the Near East, and much of what had been done was concerned principally with recovering works of Islamic art or with major architectural monuments. Beginning in the 1970s, however, there was an explosion of archaeological exploration conducted along broader lines (often with an anthropological focus), especially in Syria, Jordan, Israel and Turkey, with important work also undertaken in Iran, Egypt, Lebanon and Yemen. This work has helped correct serious misconceptions about the historical evolution of the Levant, in particular, during the early Islamic period. For example, it had earlier been the norm to assume that the rise of Islam coincided with a general collapse of prosperity, but the careful work of Donald Whitcomb, Alan Walmsley and others[17] revealed that many areas in the Levant continued to flourish during the seventh century and into the eighth. Numerous buildings once considered to date from the end of the Byzantine period were reassigned, on the basis of more careful stratigraphy and better knowledge of the ceramic sequences, to the early Islamic period. The rise of Islam, rather than being seen as an episode of violent destruction and discontinuity, appeared instead to be what one scholar called an 'invisible conquest',[18] because at most sites in the Levant the transition from Byzantine to Islamic rule was so gradual as to be imperceptible, at least in terms of the archaeological evidence – in contrast to the image gained from literary sources, both Christian and Islamic.[19]

This burst of new work, then, utilising new kinds of evidence beyond the Arabic literary sources, ushered in nothing less than a revolution in our understanding of early Islam; and the new evidence, and novel interpretations of long-known literary evidence, resulted in the appearance of many new attempts to reconstruct 'what actually happened' at Islam's origins. It is impossible to provide a comprehensive overview here of all the works and new ideas that formed part of the 'revisionist wave'; but in what follows, I will try briefly to highlight a few themes as illustrative of the variety of viewpoints that have been advanced as part of the revisionist wave – almost all of them in sharp contrast to the views of the traditional paradigm.

One novel approach has been to deny that what we call the

rise of Islam began as a unified movement at all. The historian Moshe Sharon in the mid-1980s, for example, posited that there was an indigenous Arabian form of indeterminate monotheism – indeterminate meaning that it was not Judaism or Christianity – that existed before Muhammad. These monotheists formed communities in various parts of the Arabian peninsula, each under a different leader. One was led by Muhammad but, as Sharon put it, 'about the nature of Muhammad's activity we can only guess'. In time these different communities of monotheists expanded into Syria and Iraq, and through a process of sorting out in the 650s (what the traditional paradigm would recognise as the first *fitna* or civil war), there emerged a unified state led by the Umayyads, and this later unity was projected backwards and given a supposed unified origin in Muhammad's leadership.[20]

Perhaps the most extreme position has been to assert that Muhammad never actually existed, a hypothesis sometimes building on the fact that the name of Muhammad is not found in Muslim coins and inscriptions until the second half of the seventh century. Volker Popp, relying heavily on numismatic evidence, presented a reconstruction according to which Arabic-speaking Nestorian Christian contingents of the Sasanian military, held in reserve when the Sasanian forces were defeated by the Byzantines in 627–8 CE, launched a counter-offensive against the Byzantines, whom they detested for their long persecution of Nestorian Christians. They persuaded other disaffected Christian groups such as the Miaphysite Christians of Syria and Egypt to join them, chased the Byzantines out of the Levant and Egypt, and established a new state. The Umayyads, in this presentation, thus began as Nestorian Christians.[21] Yehuda Nevo proposed a different hypothetical reconstruction that also dispensed with the presence of Muhammad entirely. According to Nevo, the Byzantine emperors grew weary of the religious fractiousness of the provinces of Syria and Egypt, and so planned to set up friendly Arab dynasties there and hand power over to them. This, they hoped, would spare them the nuisance of having to manage these troublesome areas; but after they voluntarily withdrew, their former clients assumed a hostile attitude, and emerged as the Umayyad state, which launched raids against the Byzantines and even twice besieged the Byzantine capital at Constantinople.[22] I will not discuss these and other such hypotheses further here, but will simply say that they seem to me to pose greater problems than they solve. For one thing, although it is true that Muhammad is not mentioned in any document produced by the Believers themselves so far discovered, these theories must pass in silence over the fact that some quite early non-Muslim sources do mention Muhammad, so their effort to erase him from the historical record seems high-handed. Moreover, the idea (in Popp's scenario) that Nestorian Christians would have been able to win the support of Miaphysites in their campaign against the Chalcedonian Byzantines seems dubious, given the fact that the Nestorians and Miaphysites considered each other, as well as Chalcedonian Christians, to be heretics and had spent more than a century attacking one another in very pointed polemics. And, it is hard to believe that the Byzantine emperors ever contemplated withdrawing voluntarily from provinces they controlled – in the case of Egypt, an economically vital province at that. In comparison to such hypotheses, Crone and Cook's reconstruction in *Hagarism* seems positively tame, as they hewed much closer to the existing sources and always accepted the existence of Muhammad as a historical figure.

In recent years, some scholars have attempted to imply, or to assert outright, that Islam began as a form of Christianity. We have seen that one of the early revisionist writers, Günter Lüling, considered Muhammad's movement as having started in a Christian environment in Mecca. The notion that Christianity is somehow to be found at the root of Islam has not infrequently been held, however, by those who, unlike Lüling, wish to deny the existence of Muhammad (as we saw in the case of Popp, mentioned above). Christoph Luxenberg, the apparent leader of a coterie of scholars who rather presumptuously style themselves the 'Inarah' or 'Enlightenment' group, has argued that the mosaic inscriptions in the Dome of the Rock, built by the Umayyad 'Abd al-Malik in the 690s, demonstrate that Islam was originally a Christian movement. As is well known, the mosaics on the inside of the Dome contain many verses from the Qur'an. According to Luxenberg, however, the references in those inscriptions (and in the Qur'an) to 'Muhammad, the apostle of God' (*rasul Allah*) really refer to Jesus, who elsewhere in the inscriptions (and the Qur'an) is also called *rasul Allah*. The word *muhammad*, in Luxenberg's view, is actually not the name of a person as we have thought for centuries, but is the Arabic rendering of a Syriac word meaning 'the highly praised one', so that the phrase *muhammad rasul Allah* should be understood to mean 'the highly praised apostle of God', a reference to Jesus.[23] This theory, like those just discussed, ignores the testimony of the early non-Muslim sources mentioned above, which do mention Muhammad. It also raises other problems: for instance, the Dome of the Rock inscriptions also roundly denounce the concept of the Trinity, which means that these supposed Christian inscriptions must come from non-Trinitarian Christians, who are, however, unknown in geographical Syria at this time.

Another trend in some revisionist scholarship has been to dismiss the role of Islam, or of religion of any form, in the expansion movement of the seventh century, and to understand the expansion instead as a manifestation of some kind of 'Arab' identity. Actually, this idea is a very old one, as I noted in my opening comments, advanced already in the late nineteenth century by scholars such as Hugo Winckler (who imputed climatic change in Arabia as the force that drove the 'Arabs' from the peninsula). It is an idea encapsulated and popularised in the term 'the Arab conquest' for the expansion of Islam. The notion that the expansion was the result of climate change was discredited long ago, but some revisionist writers rehabilitated the view that the expansion was essentially a national or ethnic one in more subtle terms. Patricia Crone herself seems to have been attracted to this view, for her book *Meccan Trade and the Rise of Islam* (1987) includes an extended discussion of the idea that Islam began as a 'nativist' movement against Byzantine encroachment.[24] More detailed was the presentation by the Palestinian scholar Suliman Bashear (1947–91), whose book *Arabs and Others in Early Islam* argued that the 'Arab state' was established first, after which Islam as a religion developed to legitimate the state in the religious context of the Near East.[25] More recently, others have attempted to reinforce the notion that the rise of Islam began as an expression of a presumed 'Arab' identity.[26] We cannot here provide a full critique of this idea, but basically there seems to be no substantial evidence for the existence of an Arab political identity on the eve of, or at the time of, the rise of Islam. It therefore seems that such theories engage in the careless projection of modern nationalist notions of ethnic or national identity back to the distant past.[27]

Another tendency found in some revisionist work is the idea that Islam developed in stages, beginning with a strongly monotheistic impulse (perhaps to be identified with the elusive *ḥanifiyya* mentioned in the Qur'an, which seems to predate Muhammad)[28] and gradually acquiring more distinctive features until the lineaments of Islam as we know it become clearly established. This sometimes posits the existence of early phases in which the movement begun by Muhammad was not so sharply distinguished from other monotheist faiths. Crone and Cook, in *Hagarism*, argued that Islam began as what they termed 'Judeao-Hagarism', an early form that had close associations with Judaism.²⁹ Yehuda Nevo examined early Arabic graffiti and inscriptions in the Negev that refer not only to Muhammad but also to Moses and Jesus, suggesting a confessionally indistinct monotheism.³⁰ In my own work I have proposed that Muhammad began a movement of 'Believers' (*mu'minun*) that at first included not only those who followed the Qur'an but also other monotheists, such as Jews and Christians, who were deemed adequately righteous, and only about the year 700 CE redefined itself as the distinct monotheistic confession we know as Islam.³¹ All of these theories stand in contradistinction to the traditional paradigm, which posits that Islam as a fully developed faith distinct from other monotheisms existed from the very beginning, at the time of Muhammad.

Still another notion that has been advanced by revisionist scholars since the 1980s is the possibility that the movement begun by Muhammad, whatever we choose to call it, was apocalyptic in nature – that is, that Muhammad and his early followers were convinced that the End-Time and Last Judgement were imminent. This idea, which Muslim tradition strenuously disavows, was actually advanced forcefully as early as 1911 by the French scholar Paul Casanova in his book *Mahomet et la fin du monde*,³² but Casanova's work never gained much traction among traditional Orientalists and was quietly ignored for decades. It is, however, an idea that is once again gaining some attention, in part because of the strongly eschatological character of parts of the Qur'an, and in part because apocalyptic enthusiasm seems a possible way to explain the tremendous energy exhibited in the early stages of the Believers' expansion out of Arabia – which otherwise is difficult to understand.³³

This rapid survey has provided, I hope, some sense of the range and variety of new interpretations of Islam's origins that have been advanced since the beginnings of the revisionist wave that occurred around the time of Montgomery Watt's retirement in 1979.

Obviously, being so diverse and at times contradictory, they cannot all be correct. But they represent the first efforts, all I think sincere efforts, to replace the illusory certainty of the traditional paradigm with something more consonant with the broader (and growing) range of evidence – literary and documentary – now regarded as relevant. Some of these interpretations, as I have suggested above, appear destined to be set aside as inadequate, but the search for new ways of viewing Islam's origins will go on because there is still much that we do not understand about this process. To take one example: the relationship – theological and practical – between the early Believers and the Christians and Jews with whom they had contact in the Near East is still a matter that remains puzzling in many ways, and for which the available evidence is sometimes perplexingly contradictory. The Qur'an is often bluntly anti-Trinitarian; and yet we know that Christians often held important positions in the Umayyad state and participated in the conquests. On this and other topics, there is still much work to do, and a continuing need for creativity and deep reflection, if new interpretations are to be crafted that can win general assent.

Developments in the Study of the Qur'an

In the final section, I wish to focus on one more aspect of the study of early Islam that has changed greatly in recent years: that is our understanding of the early history of Islam's sacred scripture, the Qur'an.

The Qur'an, of course, lies at the very heart of the Islamic tradition. Its appearance constitutes the most crucial point in the account of Islam's origins, and the story of its revelation is the very basis of Islam's faith claims.

Tracing exactly how the Qur'an came to assume the form in which we know it today and have known it for centuries is therefore central to the project of attaining a historical understanding

Islam's origins. Ironically, this task was long neglected in the West and is only now beginning to be addressed systematically.

The Islamic tradition has, of course, its own narratives of how the Qur'an text developed. The most widely known, but not the sole, account states that the revelations vouchsafed to Muhammad were memorised by him and also by many of his followers piecemeal, as they arrived, and some of the faithful also wrote down parts of the revelation for their own use. Twenty-odd years after Muhammad's death, the third caliph 'Uthman, worried by the death of many Qur'an reciters, feared that some of the revelation might be lost and ordered that a definitive written copy be made. He appointed a team of trusted companions, led by Zayd ibn Haritha, to collect all known written copies and to interview everyone who had memorised parts of the revelation. These materials they edited together to form what is usually known as the "Uthmanic recension', and this has been the secure basis for the Qur'an text ever since that time in the 660s.

Like much of the traditional Islamic origins narrative, this story of the Qur'an's genesis and early development has also been challenged by Western scholars;[34] I mentioned earlier the revisionist views of the Qur'an's crystallisation advanced by Lüling and Wansbrough, to which could be added many more, including works by John Burton[35] and Christoph Luxenberg.[36] They part company not only with traditional Islamic views of the Qur'an, but also with each other, so we cannot yet speak of an emerging consensus in Western views on the Qur'an. But the most startling fact about these and other Western studies of the Qur'an text is that they have all been based on a deficient text. Explaining this, however, requires a short digression.

Western scholars of the eighteenth century and later developed a standard text-critical procedure for the study of foundational texts – whether it was the Hebrew Bible, the classics of ancient

Greek literature, the Gospels, the writings of the Church fathers or any other work of literature. The unshakeable assumption in such work is that every time a text is copied, errors are introduced into it, intentionally or unintentionally. Assuming that one does not have the author's autograph copy, the first step is to collate all the surviving manuscripts of the text in question and by studying them closely, to develop a stemma or 'family tree' laying out the relationship of all manuscripts to one another, so that one can tell which are copies of others, and which manuscripts belong to separate or 'sibling' lines of descent from a common ancestor text (perhaps now lost). With the stemma established, one can then utilise the earliest manuscripts from each line to reconstruct as accurately as possible a critical edition of the 'original text' (urtext). Only when a text is available in a critical edition of this kind, obviously, can one seriously begin to analyse the text's contents and try to understand its meaning, since before the creation of a critical edition one cannot know whether a particular passage in a given manuscript represents the actual words of the original author, or only a garbled version thereof, or worse yet, a later interpolation or insertion by someone else, having no relationship whatsoever to what the original author wrote. Adhering to this sequence of procedures – first collation of manuscripts, then determining the stemma, and finally, preparation of a critical edition – thus ensures that scholars are dealing as much as possible with an authentic version of the text as the original author composed it; and only such a critical edition can provide a secure basis on which a scholar may try to infer historical information through analysis of the text.

    Western studies of the Qur'an, however, have not followed this rigorous philological procedure. Indeed, they have essentially proceeded in reverse, in that scholars have written extensive studies on various aspects of the Qur'an text even though we have never had, and still today do not yet have, anything remotely resembling a proper critical edition of the Qur'an. We must therefore recognise that the myriad scholarly studies of various Qur'anic passages made over the past century and more (including a few by me) can only be considered provisional – pending the arrival at last of a critical edition of the text.

The lack of a critical edition of the Qur'an was not something of which scholars were unaware, of course. Already in 1834 Gustav Flügel attempted to provide a reliable edition, but the Flügel Qur'an was based on a very limited number of manuscripts and was almost immediately recognised as inadequate. The daunting prospect of attempting to collate the tens of thousands of known Qur'an manuscripts, however, meant that most Western scholars used the Flügel edition anyway, at least for about seventy-five years, as it was the only published version that Europeans considered in some way a 'standard' text. It gradually fell out of use after the appearance in 1924 of the Egyptian Qur'an produced by scholars at al-Azhar in Cairo, an edition that was superior to Flügel but was still far from a true critical edition. (It remains the most widely used edition even today.)

There was a plan, originally conceived early in the twentieth century by scholars affiliated with the Bavarian Academy of Sciences and the University of Munich, to create a true critical edition of the Qur'an – a project that by that time had become more feasible due to improvements in photographic technology. Led by Gotthelf Bergsträsser and then Otto Pretzl, in collaboration with the Australian Qur'an expert Arthur Jeffery, this team spent years in the 1930s amassing thousands of photographs on microfilm of early Qur'an manuscripts from the important libraries of Europe and from many in the Islamic world. The plan was to collate the manuscripts from the photographs and begin the process of establishing a critical edition. The project foundered, however. Bergsträsser, its brilliant prime mover, was an outspoken opponent of the Nazis, and disappeared under mysterious circumstances shortly after the Nazis took power in 1933. Pretzl continued the project, but was killed early in World War II. Jeffery, as an Australian, had no access to the archive of photographs stored in Munich once the war began in 1939. When the war ended, the scholar who had inherited the archive from Pretzl, Professor Anton Spitaler of Munich, announced that it had been destroyed in Allied bombing toward the end of the war.

The collapse of the project to create a critical edition may also have had other causes, however. Muslim tradition holds that the Qur'an exists in a limited number of what are usually called 'canonical variants'. These are said to be the different vocalisations of the text favoured by various companions of Muhammad, and are reflections of the fact that early Qur'ans were written in a highly deficient script that showed only the consonants, and sometimes did not distinguish adequately even between certain consonants. This *rasm* or consonantal skeleton could thus be vocalised in a variety of ways. Moreover, the thousands of manuscripts of the Qur'an in existence exhibit many other textual variants. The existence of these variants may have caused Pretzl, before he died, to have doubts about the feasibility of the project to create a critical edition of the Qur'an.

The result was that, after an auspicious start early in the twentieth century, critical study of the Qur'an text essentially came to a halt at mid-century. Montgomery Watt's whole scholarly career – including the years when he wrote his books on Muhammad's life, and *Bell's Introduction to the Qur'an* – was thus spent in this period when critical work on the Qur'an was essentially at a standstill, and everything was based rather trustingly on the 'Egyptian' Qur'an.

It is, however, no longer at a standstill today, and this marks another profound change in scholarship on early Islam since Watt's day. The current revitalisation of critical Qur'an scholarship is the result of three separate developments.

The first was the discovery, in 1972, of a trove of old Qur'an manuscripts, some of them evidently very early, that had been hidden away and forgotten for centuries, it seems, in the Great Mosque of San'a' in Yemen. A German team was brought in several years later to assist in conservation and cataloging of this collection, and photographs of these Qur'ans are now being studied by a team at the University of Saarbrücken. Among them is a palimpsest, the erased lower layer of writing of which seems also to be Qur'an, but the text of this lower layer contains numerous previously unknown and major variants from the 'standard' text; progress in reading and analysing this text has been glacial, but after a long wait, some results are beginning to appear.[37] It is too early to draw definitive conclusions, except to say that the new range of variants adds more complexity to the question of how the text came to be, and makes more acute the question of what a 'critical edition' would look like, or even how it could be attained.

The second development was the renewed, meticulous study of a number of very early copies of the Qur'an housed in European collections. Long known and sometimes examined by scholars in cursory fashion more or less as curiosities, they have finally begun to be scrutinised closely, particularly by François Déroche of the École Pratique des Hautes Études in Paris[38] (and now also by some of his students).[39] Déroche's initial aim has been to classify the earliest manuscripts (especially exemplars in Paris, St Petersburg and London) on the basis of all aspects of the text, including format, layout, decoration, palaeography, orthography and textual variants. Since these are generally large-format Qur'ans produced on full sheets of parchment and written in large, well-spaced script, they would have been expensive and time-consuming to produce, and the assumption is that they were the product of official workshops sponsored by the Umayyad caliphs. Déroche has begun the process of analysing them into coherent groups, each of which may correspond to the output of a particular workshop. On this basis, we may eventually be able to understand better how the text evolved in the first two Islamic centuries, whether particular workshops (or groups of scribes) were relatively more conservative or innovative in transmitting the text, and so on. It may also help to shed more light on the vexing phenomenon of variant readings. This kind of detailed work offers, I think, very exciting prospects for attaining, at last, a much better sense of how the Qur'an first developed as a text.

The third major development was the revelation by Professor Spitaler of Munich, a few years before his death, that the archive of microfilms amassed by Bergsträsser and Pretzl had not, in fact, been destroyed during World War II after all, but had been in his keeping all along.[40] Why he concealed them for a half-century remains a mystery, but he handed them over to a former colleague, Professor Angelika Neuwirth of Berlin, who then found funding for a long-term project (called the *Corpus Coranicum* project) to study these photographs, and to study texts from the sixth and seventh centuries CE that were part of the intellectual discourse of Late Antiquity amidst which the Qur'an took form – Christian, Jewish and other texts in Syriac, Greek, Arabic and other languages.

After a half-century in the shadows, then, critical Qur'an studies are now poised to make major gains – with no fewer than three separate centres (Saarbrücken, Paris and Berlin) finally focusing on detailed study of the actual early Qur'an manuscripts. It means that, at last, scholars are approaching the Qur'an in the proper way – starting by establishing a critical edition of the text on the basis of careful reading of the manuscripts, after which we can move on to analysis of the text.

As hinted at above, however, the task of creating a critical edition of the Qur'an will not be an easy one. The range of variants found in the extant manuscripts of the Qur'an (especially when we bring into consideration the early San'a' palimpsest) are considerably greater than those noted in the 'canonical variant' literature. This fact raises the possibility that the Qur'an may have circulated orally, or in part orally, long enough that discovering what Lüling called the 'Ur-Koran', the 'original' text of the Qur'an as known to Muhammad, may not be possible. Are we dealing, in fact, with a single text, or rather with a family of related texts? What is the relationship of the text's actual evolution to the traditional accounts of the Qur'an's revelation to Muhammad and transmission in the seventh century CE? How stable was the written text in the seventh century? Is there any evidence that some passages may be later interpolations in a text that is otherwise early?[41] These, and many other questions, still lack satisfactory answers; and searching for them is part of the agenda of the brave new world in the study of early Islam that has dawned since Montgomery Watt gradually withdrew from the front rank of contributing scholars in the 1980s. It is a different world than his, but one built on much surer foundations, and I have no doubt that were Watt alive today, he would share the enthusiasm now felt by many about the future prospects for work in early Islamic history.

Notes

1. W. Montgomery Watt, *Muhammad at Mecca*, Oxford, 1953; W. Montgomery Watt, *Muhammad at Medina*, Oxford, 1956; W. Montgomery Watt, *Muhammad: Prophet and Statesman*, Oxford, 1961.
2. Hubert Grimme, *Mohammed*, 2 vols, Münster, 1892–1895.
3. Fred M. Donner, *The Early Islamic Conquests*, Princeton, 1981.
4. G.-H. Bousquet, 'Une explication marxiste de l'Islam par un ecclésiastique épiscopalien', *Hespéris* 41 (1954), 231–47.
5. Albrecht Noth and Lawrence I. Conrad, *The Early Islamic Historical Tradition*, trans. Michael Bonner, Princeton, 1994.
6. Ibn Ishaq died in 768 CE.

7. Günter Lüling, *Über den Ur-Koran. Ansätze zur Rekonstruktion vorislamischer christlicher Strophenlieder im Qur'an*, Erlangen, 1974.
8. Cambridge, 1977.
9. Walter E. Kaegi, 'Initial Byzantine Reactions to the Arab Conquest', *Church History* 38 (1969), 139–49. Curiously, this work is not mentioned in *Hagarism*'s extensive bibliography.
10. In particular, devout Muslims, and those intent on discrediting Islam in order to advance the claims of their own faith (usually Christianity).
11. Edinburgh, 1988.
12. See my retrospective review in *Middle East Studies Association Bulletin* 40 (2006), 197–9.
13. Peter Brown, *The World of Late Antiquity: AD 150–750*, New York, 1971.
14. The most brilliant exception was that of Carl Heinrich Becker (1876–1933), whose *Papyri Schott-Reinhardt* (Heidelberg, 1906) was a magnificent study of Arabic papyri from the early eighth century, but Becker eventually left scholarship to become Minister of Culture in the Weimar Republic.
15. Particularly his *Arabic Papyri in the Egyptian Library*, Cairo, 1934–62, and over a dozen other publications.
16. We may note especially the work of Raif Georges Khoury, Yusuf Raghib, Werner Diem, Lucian Reinfandt and Petra Sijpesteijn, among many others.
17. To mention a few: Denis Genequand, Heinz Gaube, Michael Meinecke, Jodi Magness, Claus-Peter Haase, P. M. Watson, Robert Schick, J.-P. Sodini and Jeremy Johns.
18. Peter Pentz, *The Invisible Conquest: the Ontogenesis of Sixth and Seventh Century Syria*, Copenhagen, 1992.
19. On this problem in the literary sources, see Fred M. Donner, 'Visions of the Early Islamic Expansion: from the Heroic to the Horrific', in *Byzantium in Early Islamic Syria*, eds Nadia El-Cheikh and Shaun O'Sullivan, Beirut and Balamand, 2011, 9–29.
20. Moshe Sharon, 'The Birth of Islam in the Holy Land', in *The Holy*

Land in History and Thought, ed. Moshe Sharon, Johannesburg, 1986, 225–35. On the notion of pre-Islamic monotheism, see also the ideas of Waardenburg, cited below at note 28.

21. Volker Popp, 'Die frühe Islamgeschichte nach inschriftlichen und numismatischen Zeugnissen', in *Die dunklen Anfänge. Neue Forschungen zur Entstehung und frühen Geschichte des Islam*, eds Karl-Heinz Ohlig and Gerd-R. Puin, Berlin, 2005, 16–123.
22. Yehuda Nevo and Judith Koren, *Crossroads to Islam: the Origins of the Arab Religion and the Arab State*, Amherst, NY, 2003.
23. Christoph Luxenberg, 'Neudeutung der arabischen Inschrift im Felsendom zu Jerusalem', in *Die dunklen Anfänge*, eds Ohlig and Puin, 124–47.
24. Patricia Crone, *Meccan Trade and the Rise of Islam*, Princeton, 1987, 231–50; she explicitly begins with a critique of Watt's views.
25. Suliman Bashear, *Arabs and Others in Early Islam*, Princeton, 1997 [*Studies in Late Antiquity and Early Islam*, 8].
26. Notably Robert Hoyland, *In God's Path: the Arab Conquests and the Creation of an Islamic Empire*, New York, 2015.
27. For a fuller rebuttal, see: Fred M. Donner, 'Review of Robert Hoyland, *In God's Path*', *Al-'Usur al-Wusta: the Bulletin of Middle East Medievalists* 23 (2015), 134–40; Fred M. Donner, 'Talking About Islam's Origins', *BSOAS* 81, 1, 2018, 1–23. See also the detailed study of the question of Arab identity in relation to the rise of Islam in Peter Webb, *Imagining the Arabs: Arabic Identity and the Rise of Islam*, Edinburgh, 2016.
28. Jacques Waardenburg, 'Towards a Periodization of Earliest Islam according to its relations with Other Religions', in *Proceedings of the 9th Congress of the Union Européenne des Arabisants et Islamisants*, ed. Rudolph Peters, Leiden, 1981, 304–26; reprinted in *The Qur'an: Style and Contents*, ed. Andrew Rippin, Aldershot, 2001, 93–115.
29. Crone and Cook, *Hagarism*.
30. *Ancient Arabic Inscriptions from the Negev*, eds Yehuda D. Nevo, Zemira Cohen and Dalia Heftmann, Jerusalem, 1993.
31. Fred M. Donner, 'From Believers to Muslims: Confessional Self-

Identity in the Early Muslim Community', *Al-Abhath* 50–1 (2001–2), 9–53; Fred M. Donner, *Muhammad and the Believers: at the Origins of Islam*, Cambridge, MA, 2010.

32. Paul Casanova, *Mahomet et la fin du monde, étude critique sur l'islam primitif*, 2 vols, Paris, 1911–24.
33. See Fred M. Donner, 'Seeing Islam in Historical Perspective', 1st Annual Wadie Jwaideh Memorial Lecture, Indiana University, 4 November 2002, in *In Memoriam*, eds Zaineb Istrabadi and Melissa Drain, Bloomington, 2003, 10–32; Fred M. Donner, *Muhammad and the Believers*, 78–82; Steven J. Shoemaker, *The Death of a Prophet: the End of Muhammad's Life and the Beginnings of Islam*, Philadelphia, 2012, index s.v. 'Eschatology'.
34. Harald Motzki, 'The Collection of the Qur'an: a reconsideration of Western views in light of recent methodological developments', *Der Islam* 78 (2001), 1–34. See also Viviane Comorro, 'Pourquoi et comment le Coran a-t-il été mis par écrit?', in *Les origines du Coran, le Coran des origines*, eds François Déroche, Christian Julien Robin and Michel Zink, Paris, 2015, 191–205. Comorro shows that the story of Zayd's editorial activity is only one of several different narratives that circulated in the Islamic community on how the Qur'an assumed its present form.
35. John Burton, *The Collection of the Qur'an*, Cambridge, 1977.
36. Christoph Luxenberg, *Die syrisch-aramäische Lesart des Korans*, Berlin, 2000.
37. For example, Elisabeth Puin, 'Ein früher Koranpalimpsest aus Sanaa II (DAM 01-27.1)', in *Schlaglichter. Die beiden ersten islamischen Jahrhunderte*, eds Markus Groß and Karl-Heinz Ohlig, Berlin, 2008, 461–93; Elisabeth Puin, Teil II, *Vom Koran zum Islam*, eds Groß and Ohlig, Berlin, 2009, 523–81; Elisabeth Puin, Teil III, in *Die Entstehung einer Weltreligion I. Von der koranischen Bewegung zum Frühislam*, eds Groß and Ohlig, Berlin, 2010, 233–305; Elisabeth Puin, Teil IV, in *Die Entstehung . . . II*, eds Groß and Ohlig, Berlin, 2011, 311–99; Behnam Sadeghi and Uwe Bergmann, 'The Codex of the Companion of the Prophet and the Qur'an of the Prophet',

Arabica 57 (2010), 343–436; Behnam Sadeghi and Mohsen Goudarzi, 'San'a' 1 and the Origins of the Qur'an', *Der Islam* 87 (2012), 1–129.

38. See, among many other works, François Déroche, *Les manuscrits du Coran: aux origines de la calligraphie coranique*, Paris, 1983; François Déroche, *Qur'ans of the Umayyads: a First Overview*, Leiden, 2014.
39. See in particular the work of Eléonore Cellard, *La transmission manuscrite du Coran. Étude d'un corpus de manuscrits datables du 2ᵉ/8ᵉ siècle J. C.*: dissertation Paris: INALCO, 2015.
40. See Andrew Higgins, 'The Lost Archive', *Wall Street Journal*, 12 January 2008. Available at <http://www.wsj.com/articles/SB120008793352784631> (last accessed 28 April 2018).
41. David Powers, *Muhammad Is Not the Father of Any of Your Men*, Philadelphia, 2009, had identified a passage in which a word apparently has been altered in one of the earliest known Qur'an manuscripts.

3

Committed Openness: a Glance at William Montgomery Watt's Religious Life

Richard Holloway

The title I have given this short chapter is 'Committed Openness: a Glance at William Montgomery Watt's Religious Life'. And I think the title needs an explanation. In religion being both committed and open would be considered by many to be a contradiction in terms. There is a strong belief in both Christianity and Islam that the religious question has been fully and finally answered. The matter is closed. The revelation is sealed. All that is left is commentary, explanation and commitment. If you are open, you can't be committed. If you are committed, you can't be open. William Montgomery Watt would have smiled quietly at that and replied: 'Maybe so, but I happen to be both.'

Like many another distinguished Scot, he was a son of the manse, born on 14 March 1909 to Andrew and Mary Watt, in Ceres, Fife, where his father was minister. The most significant event in his life, when he was only fourteen months old, was the death of his father, who had just become minister of Balshagray Parish Church in Glasgow. In an unpublished manuscript from his later years William meditated on the impact his father's death had on his own attitude to life. It had necessitated a lot of moving about in his early years, and he mused: 'I sometimes wonder if this early change of abode is the source of my tendency, once I have found a tolerable billet, to remain in it as long as possible.'

He was a good example of what Hugh MacDiarmid famously described as the Caledonian Antisyzygy, the existence of two opposing or competing polarities in the same entity, the famous Scottish double-mindedness. If the search for stability of life was one of the polarities in his character, the other equally powerful drive was for intellectual and spiritual exploration. So it was that in 1937 William made a turn that would direct the rest of his life: he discovered Islam. While studying for a doctorate at Edinburgh, he took in a Muslim lodger to make ends meet, K. A. Mannan, a student from India (later Pakistan) who was a member of the Ahmadiyya sect.[1] This is how he described what happened:

> I began to learn something about Islam, of which I had been largely ignorant; but the dominant impression was that I was engaged not merely in arguing with this individual but in confronting a century-old system of thought and life.

That turn to Islam led him to correspond with the Anglican Bishop in Jerusalem, George Francis Graham Brown. Brown became something of a father figure to William, who agreed to join him in Jerusalem as his chaplain, while working on the intellectual approach to Islam. He was fast-tracked through Cuddesdon Theological College in Oxford in one year and ordained deacon in 1939. He served a curacy at St Mary's Church, The Boltons, Kensington, and began the study of Arabic at the School of Oriental and African Studies in London. He was ordained priest in 1940. When St Mary's was closed because of bomb damage, he returned to Edinburgh to finish his training as a curate at Old St Paul's

Church, where he also began work on his doctoral thesis, 'Free Will and Predestination in Early Islam'.

He finally made it to Jerusalem to work with Bishop Brown in 1943. After his return to Scotland in 1946, he was made Lecturer in Arabic at the University of Edinburgh, where he remained – another 'tolerable billet' – until retirement in 1979. He was given a Personal Chair in Arabic and Islamic Studies in 1964. William said of his commitment to the study of Islam that he always had an ability to see the other person's point of view, 'indeed almost a tendency to prefer the other's point of view'. And he became fascinated by the historical prejudice of the West against Islam.

His understanding of this prejudice was increased by his association with Norman Daniel, author of *Islam and the West: the Making of an Image*.[2] Daniel persuaded him that the distorted image of Islam in the West was created by scholars between the twelfth and fourteenth centuries to provide propaganda in support of the Crusades. William came to the conviction that the distorted image 'was a negative aspect of European identity, that is, an image of what the European is not. It is then in contrast to his positive identity as a Christian.' William then went on to say: 'The tenacity of the prejudice I would attribute to the fact that the distorted image was an essential aspect of the emergence of European identity.'

He remained a Christian, and worked for many years as a priest for the Scottish Episcopal Church, but there was a time, under the influence of Charles de Foucauld, the French priest who lived as a hermit among the Muslim desert tribes of Algeria until his assassination in 1916, when he thought of his vocation as constituting 'a willed and deliberate presence' in the intellectual world of Islam. To implement this conception of presence, William often took as the basis of his daily meditation a passage, either from the Qur'an or from an Islamic mystical work.

William brought the same exploratory reverence to his own Christian faith. He was born in the Kirk, evolved into Anglicanism, but retained enormous respect for the Presbyterian tradition – I do not think he thought very much of bishops – and he respected the decision of his wife, Jean, whom he married in 1943, to become a Roman Catholic. He joined the Iona Community in 1960, because he found its brand of radical and exploratory faith congenial. He continued to be both an explorer and a theological reconciler right up to the end. His last book, published in 2002 when he was ninety-three, was *A Christian Faith for Today*,[3] a distillation of the sort of generous Christianity to which he had given his life.

I want to conclude with an image from William's family life. He and Jean bought their first house, the Neuk, at Bridgend, Dalkeith, in 1947, and it proved to be a very tolerable billet. Then in 1956 they acquired another house in Crail, in Fife, for holidays. Those two welcoming homes supplied an almost liturgical rhythm to their family life. At Crail, during summer holidays by the sea, William worked hard to create a little beach for his five children. He moved rocks, dug channels and battled seaweed to provide them with a clear space on the rocky shore. By summer's end it would be almost perfect, but when the Watts were back in their town house in Dalkeith, the sea would destroy what he had created. And the following summer he would have to do it all over again.

It speaks of his determination, but it also speaks of something more profound. Though the struggle against it is never finished, he spent his life battling the tide of intolerance. In our time that tide is once again at flood level.

William Montgomery Watt was a theologically liberal, socially and politically radical Christian who loved Islam. As I said at the beginning: committed openness.

Notes

1. Editor's note: Watt states elsewhere in his unpublished autobiography that Mannan later became 'an ordinary Muslim'.
2. Norman Daniel, *Islam and the West: the Making of an Image*, Oxford, 2009.
3. London and New York, 2002.

PART 2

UNPUBLISHED WRITINGS OF WILLIAM MONTGOMERY WATT

4

A Diary

Editor's Preface

The wording and section titles here are copied verbatim from a photocopy of Professor Watt's handwritten diary, which he gave me some time around the year 2000.[1] The text here is presented in the order in which it appears in the diary. Sometimes a portion of the text is introduced with a title and sometimes the subject changes without a new title.

This work was written gradually. In its present form, some, though not all of it, probably dates from the 1970s. Its style is informal and its tone is personal. Its pagination is disordered and there are passages that have been written more than once, as well as earlier sections that have been deleted and replaced by fuller ones.

This unpublished text has been included here because of the valuable light it sheds on William's personality, childhood, education and early views on religion.

The Text

My mother

This is an appropriate place to give an outline of my mother's life. After her sister Jeanie's death, she was the oldest of the children, but she was able to train as a teacher, first as a 'pupil teacher' at Larkhall Academy, and then at an institution in Glasgow. She presumably completed her training before 1890, and then worked as a teacher until her marriage. She had a very fine contralto voice, and told me that she had thought of becoming a professional singer but decided that it was somewhat risky as a career.

My father and she married on 17 July 1902, after he had been minister of Ceres for a few months, and there she played a full part in local life as the minister's wife (though I think I am right in saying that at that time there were three other churches in the village). I did not appear until March 1909, but Mother was then very satisfied at having produced the first Burns grandchild.

In summer 1909 my father moved to be first minister of Balshagray Parish Church in Glasgow. Within a few months, however, he was found to be suffering from a kidney disease for which there was then no cure, and he died in May 1910.

Mother and I were then mostly with Granny and Grandpa at Woodburn, and I went to school in Larkhall in 1914. Mother was more competent than Granny at most household jobs, especially cooking, and Granny let her take the leading part, with the result that the two women worked together in complete harmony.

When I went to school in Edinburgh in summer 1919, Mother and I went to live with the Grahams, and Mother contributed by doing more than a full share of the housework. Then in 1927, with help from Grandpa, I think, Mother bought a small flat at 110 Blackford Avenue.

While I was at Edinburgh University we spent a large part of the vacations at Larkhall. After I went to Oxford in 1930, Mother and Granny were a lot together during my absences south. With my return to Edinburgh University in 1933, the outward form of life was much what it had been during my previous period there. Mother's health on the whole was very good, but she developed breast cancer. The operation was apparently successful, but the homeopathic doctor she was attending delayed the operation a little – a year or two later she developed cancer secondaries, and died on 11 March 1937. She was the first person to be buried from a new church more or less opposite our flat – the Reid Memorial – which she had almost proudly referred to as 'our little cathedral'.

My father

My father originally trained as a teacher in much the same way as Mother, but I am not sure where he taught. Latterly he was at Sciennes School, Edinburgh, for I have a book presented to him when he left in 1894. He had decided that he had a call to the ministry, and went forward to a course of theological study. His sympathies were with what has sometimes been called the 'high church' party in the Church of Scotland – those who favoured more formal types of worship than were prevalent at the time.

After completing his theological course he was first an assistant at Riccarton, near Kilmarnock. In 1902 he was appointed minister of Ceres, and after being settled in there married my mother. There he remained until September 1909, when he moved to be the first minister of Balshagray Parish Church in Glasgow, as I have mentioned above. Unexpectedly he died on 12 May 1910.

He wrote out his sermons in a form of Pitman's shorthand, and I still have several hundreds of them. I don't think he actually 'read' them, because some of them tail off at the end, and his peroration must have been extempore. While I was at school Mother encouraged me to take the shorthand class, and though I became able to write at sixty or eighty words a minute, I did not find it easy to read the sermons. Perhaps I was not sufficiently interested, or perhaps the shorthand I learned was rather more streamlined. About 1990, however, in the course of spring cleaning, my wife brought out the parcels of sermons, and I put them in chronological order and found a place for them in my study. Then I thought I would see if I could read them. Along with them was the shorthand manual my father had used, so I was surprised to find that with the help of this I was able to read them without too much difficulty. I find reading those sermons last thing at night a form of relaxing and I have continued the practice through the years, so that I have now read them several times.

This is also, of course, a kind of meditation. Most of all, however, it brings me into touch with the father I never knew. It confirms what I had learnt from Mother about his 'high church' attitude. Beyond that, however, it shows him deeply aware of social problems – more aware, I suspect, than most of his contemporaries. I feel certain he would have approved of my membership of the Iona Community. It has been strange to find him using forms of words closely resembling what I was saying half a century later. I sometimes wonder how much of my thinking is really mine and how much is my genes. The most amazing matter is that when he received the prize for ecclesiastical history in 1897 he chose – I presume he chose – Sir William Muir's *Life of Mahomet*. There are some sentences in the sermons showing a positive attitude to other religions, especially Buddhism. My mother, who was very musical, was somewhat amused at his complete lack of musical talent.

My university education

In October 1927 I started on a course of Honours MA in Classics at Edinburgh University. Because I had deferred my entry from 1926 to 1927, I decided to complete the course in three years instead of four. This was not difficult since the actual Latin and Greek classes only covered three years, but it meant that I had to do political economy as my 'compulsory outside subject' instead of philosophy or moral philosophy as I would have preferred. I also had a short course in classical art from David Talbot-Rice. In my third year there were only the Latin and Greek courses.

In December 1929 I went to Oxford to sit an examination, and was fortunate in securing the Warner Exhibition at Balliol College. I took up residence at Balliol (in the college itself) in October 1930, and started to work for the degree of Litterae Humaniores, usually known as 'Greats'. The work consisted of philosophy (with the emphasis on Greek) and ancient history (that is, Greek and Roman), and involved considerable use of Latin and Greek texts. I went to various lectures, as directed by my tutors. (Oxford lectures were less directly related to the degree than Edinburgh ones.) In summer 1932 I realised that I was not quite ready for the degree exam, but was urged by my tutors to go ahead. It was not altogether surprising that I only achieved a second. As my exhibition had another year to run, I decided to work for a BPhil. I gained the degree in summer 1933 and graduated both BA and BPhil that year. Both Mother and Granny were at the graduation.

In the autumn[2] I started to work for a PhD at Edinburgh University. My supervisor was Norman Kemp Smith, Professor of Logic and Metaphysics, and the subject he suggested and I accepted was 'The Factual and the Problematic'. I think I attended some of his lectures and possibly also some of A. E. Taylor's (the Professor of Moral Philosophy) but I do not remember clearly. I went to Jena for the summer semester 1934 and stayed with a German family, that of the Secretary of the University. I attended philosophy lectures at the university, where one of the main professors was Bruno Bauch.[3]

In October 1934 I began work as an assistant to A. E. Taylor in the Moral Philosophy Department. I had had the possibility of an assistant lectureship at the University of Bangor in Wales, but I chose Edinburgh. This appointment as an assistant was limited to three years and was not renewable. I was given an extension for a fourth year, partly, I think, because of my mother's death. After that I had to find another post, and there were few lectureships open. The chief possibility was a post at Scots Church College, Calcutta, with the title of 'professor'. I would probably have got this, if I had applied – it was open for a long time; but before I had to make the decision, another element had come into my life.

Before describing this in detail it will be helpful to say something about my religious life. On returning to Edinburgh in 1933 I attended St Giles on Sundays as I had previously. Almost opposite our flat, however, a splendid new church was built, the Reid Memorial. After it opened – late 1936, I think – we went there instead of St Giles. After Mother's death on 11 March 1937, Granny then kept house for me until the end of the summer term. From October, however, I had to have a housekeeper. In order to pay for her I asked a friend to come to stay as a paying guest. This friend was K. A. Mannan, an Indian (later Pakistani) Muslim studying veterinary medicine whom I had got to know at a society for overseas people which met at New College on Friday evenings. When Mannan, as he called himself, came to stay we tended to have long discussions over breakfast and supper about religion. He was then a member of the Ahmadiyya sect, though later he became an ordinary Muslim. In the course of these discussions I came to feel that I was confronting not just an individual but a whole tradition of thought.

After my membership of the SCM (the Student Christian Movement) in Oxford I joined up in Edinburgh. In October 1934 I was made leader of an SCM Study Group on Germany (where Hitler was gaining in power). My co-leader was Jean Donaldson,[4] who had spent the previous year in Germany as part of her degree course.

After Mother's death I felt I was not getting sufficient spiritual sustenance from the Reid Memorial Church. The basic thought was that the Eucharist should be the central service every Sunday, since sermons often stirred up intellectual questionings. (Some of this may have been inherited 'physically' from my father whose sermons show that he attached great importance to the Lord's Supper.) I decided I would join the Scottish Episcopal Church, and in particular go to Old St Paul's. I had been taken there by my friend Walter. On his advice I turned to Canon Norman Cockburn, Vice-Principal of the theological college, and he prepared me for my confirmation which took place at Old St Pauls on Whitsunday, 12 May, because he thought that it should not be delayed; I went on seeing him afterwards.

Through Norman Cockburn I heard that the Anglican Bishop in Jerusalem, George Francis Graham Brown, was wanting someone to work on the Christian approach to Islam. This sounded more interesting than teaching philosophy in Calcutta. I met the bishop while he was on holiday at St Andrews, and I went to London to talk to J. G. Matthew, the secretary of the Jerusalem and the East Mission, who was very sympathetic. I now committed myself to going to Jerusalem and forgot about Calcutta. I had first, however, to take a theological course and be ordained, since I had to be able to conduct services in Palestine.

At some date (in 1937) I submitted my thesis for the PhD and was greatly dismayed to have it rejected. I was not even given the option of revising and resubmitting it; and this last was a bit unfair, I think – and I can now speak as one who was later chairman of the PhD Committee for a year or two. I realise, however, that I did not make nearly sufficient use of my supervisor; in particular, I should have submitted specimen chapters to him for his comments. My general idea was that I was supposed to work almost entirely on my own. If the thesis had been accepted, there might have been more chance of a philosophy job in Britain.

1938–46 To Jerusalem and back
To prepare for ordination I went to Cuddesdon College for session 1938–9 (including a fourth term in later summer). This was on the advice of Norman Cockburn, who thought it would be better for me than his own college. Cuddesdon is a small village seven miles out of Oxford. While at Cuddesdon I met the wife of a local farmer who had been a girlfriend (but not too intimate) of T. E. Lawrence. I also consulted Professor H. A. R. Gibb of Oxford (later Sir Hamilton Gibb) about Islamic Studies. I duly passed my General Ordination Examination without much difficulty and was ready to be ordained. At Cuddesdon all the students were required to be at Mattins at an early hour but were not required to be at the Eucharist which followed. For a few days I hesitated about the latter, but then decided to become a daily communicant.

I had hoped to get a curacy in Oxford but found none, and instead went to St Mary, The Boltons, Kensington, London. The vicar was George Bosworth, and he and his wife put me up for my first year. I was ordained on 29 September in St Pauls Cathedral by the Bishop of Willesden (as the bishopric of London was vacant). I think the service took place in the large crypt, because the Second World War had started. In arranging to go to London I had hoped to take up the study of Arabic there. Because of the war, however, the School of Oriental Studies had moved to Cambridge but the vicar allowed me to go to Cambridge from Monday to Friday for the rest of 1937. There I began the study of Arabic, chiefly under Professor Tritton, though I think I also got something from my late colleague, Laurence Elwell-Sutton. After January I continued to study Arabic on my own as far as time permitted; and I had one or two contacts with a member of the SOS[5] staff about a possible thesis; but nothing came of this.

I was ordained priest on 2 October 1940 and two days later George Bosworth went off as a padre, leaving me in charge of the parish. I moved to a couple of rooms in Church House in Redcliffe Gardens. On my first Sunday evening in charge I was raised from bed with word that the church was on fire. There had been an air raid and five bombs had fallen on the church roof. One made a hole in the roof of the vestry and caused a little damage, but another went through the roof above the Lady Chapel and made rather a mess there. There was no real fire, however. After that we had bombs in the parish most nights that week, but after that virtually nothing, though there were raids round about. I slept in the basement of Church House along with the caretaker and his wife. I also became an air raid warden and went round a number of streets to make sure no lights were showing. When the church roof was examined for possible damage, it was found that, though there none from the bombing, there was a considerable amount of dry rot in the beams; and it was decided to close the church.

I was fortunate in being accepted as a curate at Old St Paul's Church, Edinburgh, by the rector Peter Monie, and I moved to Edinburgh in February 1941. After London Edinburgh felt a haven of peace. I remained as a curate at Old St Paul's until after Easter 1943. During this period I was able to resume my Arabic studies under Dr Richard Bell at Edinburgh University and began to work on a PhD under his supervision on 'Free Will and Predestination in Early Islam'. This was meant to fit in with work in Cairo and Jerusalem organised by Constance Padwick, with whom I was in contact through Kitty Henry in London. None of the other parts of the scheme ever came to anything. When I left Old St Paul's in April 1943 it was largely with a view to marriage, and in fact Jean and I were married in St Luke's, Redcliffe Square, London (which had taken over from St Mary's, since the latter was officially closed) on 15 May. I was also waiting for a passage to the Middle East. I went to live with Jean at her digs at Lathbury, just outside Newport Pagnell – she was doing war work at Bletchley. While there I completed my PhD thesis, though I could not officially submit it until the following summer.

The awaited passage eventually came, and at the end of November I sailed from Glasgow, Jean seeing me off. Because of war conditions, we sailed in a slow convoy of about forty ships, making a long detour into the Atlantic, and not reaching Port Said until 31 December. Then we had to go to Cairo, and I did not reach Jerusalem until 6 January 1944.

In Jerusalem I continued my Arabic studies under the Danish pastor Alfred Nielsen and a Mrs Wakely. I also continued Islamic studies, but I think I spent rather more time on what might be called the Christian background of Islam. I wrote most of a longish book which has never been published, since my hopes of cooperation with an ecclesiastical historian have never been fulfilled. There is a short summary of some of my conclusions in the first chapter of *Muslim–Christian Encounters*.

Apart from study, my duties consisted in taking services at St Luke's Hospital, Hebron. And in the Anglican Church in Jaffa, roughly on a fortnightly basis. I also took services in Beirut in July 1945, including the VE Day service. For this period Jean and I made our base in the Friends' School – she had been able to join me in November 1944. Our daughter Ann was born in November 1945.

Bishop Graham Brown had been killed in a motor accident in 1941 or 1942, and his successor – Wesley Henry Stewart – was not so keen – I felt – on the Islamic work. This work was also limited by the fact that there was no institution of higher Islamic education in Palestine. These factors, I think, more than the deteriorating political situation, led me to decide not to return to Jerusalem for a fourth 'tour'. My original 'tour' had been for three years (less three months), but when a passage home became available in August 1946 the bishop allowed us to take it. Before we left we heard the blowing up of the King David Hotel (which included government offices) by Jewish terrorists, and we knew several of those killed, especially Brian Gibbs, whose posthumous daughter Catherine is our godchild. We left our belongings in Jerusalem, as it was difficult to make decisions in the middle of all the tensions there; but on the boat home we decided definitely not to return.

Soon after reaching Edinburgh at the end of August 1946 I went to see Professor John Macmurray to ask if there was any possibility of a job, and was told that the Lecturer in Ancient Philosophy had died a week or two earlier and they had no hope of a replacement. This was a post for which I was well qualified. When I went to see the other Professor A. D. Ritchie he was assuming that I would be taking the job. And so I returned Edinburgh University. For a bit we lived with Jean's mother at 14 Warrender Park Terrace.

At the end of the session 1946–7 Richard Bell retired and I applied for the Arabic lectureship and was appointed. From October 1947 I was in charge of Arabic and Islamic Studies until I retired at the end of September 1979. But this concluding stage of my life will require separate and different treatment.

Following on from my appointment to Arabic we bought our house at the Neuk, Bridgend, Dalkeith. We moved in about the end of March 1947. It is an old house with a built-in sundial dated 1753; but parts of the house are probably even older, as it has been added to and altered in various ways. We too have altered it. We made what is now my study from what we found as a washhouse and coal cellar with a separate entrance, and we had to make an entrance from the rest of the house with seven steps.[6]

Notes

1. Occasionally extra punctuation has been added.
2. This part of the diary is dated 7 November 1997.
3. A German Neo-Kantian philosopher.
4. This is the person who would become Professor Watt's wife.
5. The earlier name – the School of Oriental Studies in London – was later changed to the School of Oriental and African Studies.
6. The narrative stops abruptly here.

5

'The Testament of a Search' and Later Unpublished Writings

Editor's Preface

Professor Watt wrote a more lengthy text, 'The Testament of a Search'. It was never published and it remains in typewritten form only. It is a second autobiographical study. Composed later than his handwritten diary, this later account contains valuable extra information and its tone is more formal and more reflective than its predecessor.

The Text

I was born in 1909 in the Manse of Ceres in the 'Kingdom of Fife'. My father, Andrew Watt, who came of Lanarkshire farming stock, was parish minister there. My mother, Mary, was the elder surviving daughter of John Campbell Burns, a building contractor, who liked to describe himself as a 'self-made man' and was proud to be a Justice of the Peace and county councillor. His father was a ship's captain based in Glasgow, but the unsettled circumstances of such a life made it desirable that young John should be sent to live with his grandfather, the 'dominie' or schoolteacher of the mining village of Larkhall. After his schooling he learnt the trade of a joiner, and by his intelligence and hard work and upright character became one of the leading men of the community. The family was not directly related to Robert Burns, the poet, but the anecdote was handed down in the family of how my grandfather was once told by his great-grandmother (whose husband had been a burgess of Kilmarnock) that she has once entertained the poet to tea in Kilmarnock.

When I was about six months old my father moved to Glasgow to be the minister of a new parish there. I sometimes wonder if this early change of abode is the source of my tendency, once I have found a billet, to remain in it as long as possible. This change, however, was soon to be followed by other cataclysmic ones. When I was fourteen months old my father died after an illness of only a month or two, leaving my mother a widow of thirty-nine, and myself an only child. This experience, traumatic for both my mother and myself, has undoubtedly been a major determinant of many aspects of my later life, though it is only within the last ten years that I have appreciated its importance.

Partly in order to keep her furniture my mother rented a house, latterly at Rothesay on the island of Bute. This was useful for holidays for ourselves and my grandparents, and at other times it was let. Apart from holidays, however, we lived with the grandparents in Larkhall, and there I went to primary school, commencing my attendance just about the time of the outbreak of the First World War in August 1914. The war did not affect my life greatly at this age, but there were certain hardships and constant 'home front' efforts on behalf of the fighting men. My mother's eldest brother, James Golder Burns, served in France for most of the war as a chaplain (and published some of his impressions under the title

Through a Padre's Spectacles). We also had contacts with more distant relatives in the forces.

After the war my mother pushed ahead with the plan she had for my education, and in September 1919 I entered George Watson's College in Edinburgh, where I spent eight happy and successful years. During the school terms my mother and I lived in Edinburgh with her sister and brother-in-law, though we spent most of the holidays at my grandfather's house at Larkhall. This manner of life produced a certain sense of rootlessness, or of being an 'outsider', not fully at home either at Larkhall or in Edinburgh (except at school). My uncle, John Keddie Graham, was a minister of the United Free Church of Scotland and something of a scholar. As he had no children of his own, he became a kind of father to me; but my favourite uncle was always my mother's fourth brother, Bob, although I also admired her minister brother James, and latterly grew closer to him. I think it was largely because these two minister uncles were known as Golder Burns and Keddie Graham respectively, that I decided to use my middle name Montgomery, which I had inherited from my paternal grandfather. It was towards the end of my schooldays that I began to use it. When I re-joined the staff of Edinburgh University in 1946, there was Distinguished Professor Hugh Watt, to whom many of my letters went, and in self-defence I insisted on the Montgomery. When I became known as an Islamic scholar it was as Montgomery Watt, and so I am constrained to retain this form despite some disadvantages.

By the time I was fifteen my chief ambition was to become a scientist, probably one working on the theory of the atom and the subatomic entities. I insisted on following a course that would at least keep open the possibility of becoming a scientist. At the age of sixteen, however, I was persuaded to give up this idea. The uncles I have mentioned and other friends who had been at university were familiar only with arts courses, and we knew no one who had become a scientist. My headmaster was a classicist, and there were no careers masters at that time. Perhaps I myself found it difficult to find a connection between school chemistry and physics and the theoretical issues in which I was interested. So, in 1925 I abandoned science and the idea of becoming a scientist.

In accordance with the Scottish tradition I continued to study mathematics and English, as well as the classics, but it was virtually decided at this time that, when I went to the university, I should opt for the classics, at least in the first place. The road of classical scholarship was a well-trodden one, and was also well endowed with scholarships. This last was an important consideration, since my mother's finances were exiguous and there was no general system of student grants at this period. I thus became reconciled to the plan of studying Latin and Greek for the next five or six years, though I had no intention of devoting the rest of my life to this field. Already I was trying to work out ways of switching from Classics to philosophy. I did not really know what philosophy consisted in, but I surmised that the pursuit of philosophy would enable me to satisfy some of the interests that had made me want to become a scientist.

I went up to the University of Edinburgh in October 1927 and spent three years in obtaining the degree of MA with Honours in Classics. This was a four-year course but I managed to cram it into three parts. I had had an opportunity of entering the university in 1926, but decided not to forego my last year at school. It was partly to compensate for this delay that I compressed the Classics course into three years. I was also in a hurry to get to Oxford and philosophy.

I collected sufficient scholarships to enable me to go to Oxford, and in 1930 entered Balliol College as a 'late exhibitioner'. I at once entered the 'honours school of Litterae Humaniores' where the main subjects of study were philosophy (with emphasis on

Plato and Aristotle) and ancient Greek and Roman history. This was the normal continuation of the study of Latin and Greek, for it presupposed the ability to read these languages fluently. In this way I had at last reached my aim of studying philosophy. Up to this point everything had gone according to plan, or even better than plan; but a setback came in summer 1932 when I failed to get a first in Lit. Hum. and had to content myself with a second. My scholarships enabled me to spend another year at Balliol, however, and in this year I completed a thesis for the degree of BLitt on the subject of 'Kant's View of the Relation between Teleology and Ethics'. My supervisor was Clement C. J. Webb, and I enjoyed both working under his direction and also the cycle rides out through what was then country to his cottage in Marston. The BLitt to some extent compensated for the second: and three degrees in six years, instead of eight or nine, was an unusual achievement. I owe a great deal to Oxford in scholarship and other things, and yet I am also aware of it as very English and therefore 'foreign'.

In October 1933 I returned to Edinburgh University and began to work for a doctorate under the supervision of Norman Kemp Smith, Professor of Logic and Metaphysics. I wanted a subject that had some slight relevance to my underlying interest in the question of science and religion, so Kemp Smith suggested as the title 'The Factual and the Problematic', and encouraged me to begin by reading some of the works of a French philosopher of science, Emil Meyerson. During the winter of 1933–4 I attended some of Kemp Smith's lectures in Edinburgh, and then went off for the summer semester to the University of Jena, where I attended various lectures on philosophy and got to know the widow and daughter of the well-known Rudolf Eucken.[1] This was at the beginning of the Hitler period, and there were some alarms and excursions while I was in Germany. I saw some of the outward manifestations of

Hitlerism and became aware of its quasi-religious character, but saw nothing of its demonic side.

Before I returned to Scotland I had the offer of three jobs. I accepted an assistantship to the Professor of Moral Philosophy at Edinburgh, A. E. Taylor, the noted Platonic scholar. My work consisted chiefly in marking essays and conducting tutorials in which the students had an opportunity of discussing questions raised by the professor's lectures. Very occasionally there was the opportunity of lecturing. I enjoyed this work and was stimulated by it to think about ethical questions. A by-product of this thinking and of a study group on pacifism was my first published work entitled *Can Christians be Pacifists?* which came out in February 1937.[2] I often omit this title from my list of publications because it makes people think that I was and am a pacifist, which I never have been. The book is in fact a vigorous – though, as I now see, somewhat academic – critique of pacifism. It brought me a kind personal letter form William Temple, then Archbishop of York.

The publication of this book and the letter from William Temple came as a ray of light in a very gloomy period of my life. I was able to present my mother with the first fruits of all her labours on my behalf, but a few days later she died. Some months earlier a girlfriend had more or less finally rejected me. The doctoral thesis had been rejected and I had not even been given a chance of revising it. As I look back on this last matter now, I consider I was both badly advised and also somewhat unfairly treated – and I can now speak from the experience of having supervised many theses and having been convener of the committee in charge of postgraduate work in the Faculty of Arts in Edinburgh. The rejection of the thesis also adversely affected my chances of obtaining a lectureship in philosophy in a British university. The assistantships in philosophy in the Scottish universities at that time were a kind of 'dead end job', since there were far more fewer appointments in the next grade, that of lecturer. My thoughts were turning to a philosophy post in Calcutta when through a concatenation of events I found myself moving in a completely different direction.

After my mother's death I continued to live in the flat we had had, and my grandmother kept house for me until the summer vacation. For the beginning of the new session in October I decided to engage a housekeeper, and in order to pay her, since my salary was not large, I asked a friend to come as a paying guest. This friend was K. A. Mannan, a veterinary student from what later became Pakistan, and a keen and argumentative Muslim of the Ahmadiyya sect. Nearly every day we had vigorous discussions over breakfast and supper. I began to learn something about Islam, of which I had previously been largely ignorant; but the dominant impression was that I was engaged not merely in arguing with this individual but in confronting a whole century-old system of thought and life. Precisely at this juncture I was informed – by Norman Cockburn, I think – that an Anglican missionary society was looking for someone to work at the intellectual approach to Islam. Especially in the light of my association with Mannan this sounded more attractive than teaching philosophy in Calcutta, and by a roundabout route I began to make inquiries.

Before long I discovered that the society with this particular concern was the Jerusalem and the East Mission. Early in the Christmas vacation I had a very satisfactory interview with the London secretary, J. G. Matthew, and, though I was not yet committed to accept this appointment, I did nothing further about Calcutta or any other post. I began to correspond with George Francis Graham Brown, the Bishop in Jerusalem, under whom I would be working. When I met him in Scotland in August 1938, I was impressed by his great spiritual depth. In different ways both he and Mr Matthew, a retired Sudanese civil servant, were ideal father figures for me; and when my appointment at Edinburgh

University came to an end in summer 1938 I set about realising the plan that had been agreed with them. In some ways, the plan was a rather ambitious one. Though I was nearly thirty and knew no Arabic and very little about Islam, I was proposing to make myself a specialist in both Arabic and Islamics.

The first part of the plan was a year's theological course, since, if the bishop was to employ me, I must be able to conduct services, and that meant ordination. I was not averse to this step, for, as a schoolboy and later, I had sometimes thought I would like to be a minister, but had been persuaded – probably wisely – that I was too academic. The new context, however, removed that objection. For my theological studies I went to Cuddesdon College, just outside Oxford, and had an enjoyable and fruitful year. One of the highlights of the year was a meeting with the mother of T. E. Lawrence, arranged by the wife of a farmer in Cuddesdon who had known him as a schoolboy. My last few days were enlivened by the arrival of the evacuees from London at the beginning of the Second World War.

The next part of the plan was to spend two years in a curacy near a university where I could learn Arabic. I found one in London – at St Mary's, The Boltons, South Kensington, where George Bosworth was vicar – but by the time I reached London in October 1939 the war had begun and the School of Oriental Studies had moved from London to Cambridge. I was able, however, to attend a concentrated first course in Arabic by going to Cambridge for seven weeks from Monday to Friday and spending the weekends in London. Afterwards I carried on by myself to a slight extent, but progress was slow. In October 1940, just after I was ordained priest, the vicar went off as a padre leaving me in charge of the parish. On my first Sunday of full responsibility I was roused from bed about 11.30 p.m. with word that the church was on fire. There had been two fire bombs on it, but they had quickly burnt themselves out, causing more mess than damage. There were bombs in the parish on three or four nights that week, but after that we had no more. There was only a handful of a congregation left, however, and the church had been slightly damaged by a landmine a block away; so it was decided to close the church until the end of hostilities. I therefore left London in February 1941.

As it was impossible at this period of the war to travel to Palestine, I had accepted the offer of a curacy at Old St Paul's, Edinburgh. The rector was now Peter Monie, a remarkable man, who after a distinguished career in the Indian Civil Service had spent ten years as organising secretary of Toc H before seeking ordination. Life in Edinburgh was relatively peaceful after the tensions of wartime London. The most important result of the move to Edinburgh, however, was that I was able to resume my Arabic studies seriously, and in particular to commence work on a doctoral thesis on 'Free Will and Predestination in Early Islam'. The topic was chosen to fit in with some studies planned in Jerusalem, about which I had heard in correspondence with Constance Padwick.[3] My supervisor and teacher was Richard Bell, Reader in Arabic at Edinburgh University, a fine scholar of the old Scottish type.

By 1943 there were beginning to be prospects of a passage to the Middle East, and I therefore resigned from Old St Paul's after Easter. In May 1943 I married Jean Donaldson, and we spent the next six months at Newport Pagnell, where she was engaged in war work. I finished my thesis and then waited for the passage – I had to be ready at a few days' notice. The notice eventually came at the end of November. The voyage from the Clyde to Port Said in convoy lasted twenty-eight days. I reached Cairo on 31 December and Jerusalem (by train) on 6 January 1944. Jean was able to join me in November that year.

Unfortunately, about a year before my arrival Bishop Graham Brown had been killed in an accident; in the blackout his car had been hit by a train at a level crossing. I got on well with his successor, Weston Henry Stewart, but he had no special ideas about the Islamic side of the work, and I had not sufficient assertiveness to develop in the Jerusalem setting an 'intellectual approach to Islam'. I continued my study of Arabic and Islamics and did a number of small jobs; but very little of it was the intellectual work in which I had been originally interested. Jerusalem, indeed, was not well situated for such work, since there was no institution of higher education for Arabs apart from a teachers' training college. With 1946 and VE Day the political situation in Palestine worsened. I was still in Jerusalem when Jewish terrorists blew up part of the King David Hotel and killed many British officials. My tour of three years (less home leave) was almost up, and when a passage home became available in August 1946 I was allowed to take it. For some months I had been wondering whether to sign on for a second tour; but we decided that because of the tense atmosphere in Jerusalem it would be unwise to make a firm choice before we left. In the relative peace of the voyage home, however, the issues became clearer; and a week or two after reaching Edinburgh, where we stayed with Jean's mother, I decided not to return to Jerusalem.

The basic reason for the decision was my dissatisfaction with the opportunities offered by Jerusalem for the sort of work in which I was interested. The decision was made easier, however, by the fact that an appointment at Edinburgh University was almost thrust upon me. The lectureship in ancient philosophy had unexpectedly become vacant by death about the middle of August, and at this point in the university year it was virtually impossible to fill it with someone who would be free in October. The two professors of philosophy, John Macmurray and A. D. Ritchie, therefore almost pushed me into it. I was appointed for one year in the first place, but could presumably have had a permanent appointment had I so desired. My ambition to be a philosopher, however, had now been transmuted into one to work at 'the intellectual approach to Islam'. Richard Bell was to retire in summer 1947, and I applied for the post and received the appointment. This was an easier decision than some of the others I had taken previously, and events have proved its wisdom. I have become widely known among both Western and other Islamic scholars through my books on the life of Muhammad and other Islamic subjects. I have now many Muslim friends with whom I can talk freely about religious matters. I have certainly achieved more than I had any right to expect when I first opted for the Islamic field in 1938.

I began the teaching of Arabic at Edinburgh University in October 1947, and have continued there ever since as lecturer, senior lecturer, reader and finally, since 1964, as professor (with a personal chair). In this period the Arabic Department has been expanded, and Persian and Turkish have been added. The number of students has not increased dramatically, except that of Muslim postgraduates. I have published several books and numerous articles on Islamic subjects, mostly in the fields of religion and history. At the same time my intellectual immersion, as it were, in Islam has stimulated me to reflect on various problems concerned with religion or the relation between religion and the sciences. I have even had some books published in this field, though they have received much less attention than my books on strictly Islamic subjects. In this present work I am trying to give some idea of the directions in which these reflections have led me.

During these twenty-seven years I have had a very happy family life, which has had some of the usual ups and downs but which has not been seriously disturbed. The daughter born in Jerusalem has been joined by a son and three more daughters, of whom the youngest is now at university. This secure base in my home has been an important factor in all that I have achieved.

Later Unpublished Writings

i. The multiplicity of religions

Most Christians believe that the Bible is unique and that Christianity is unique, but few have looked at the matter deeply in the context of our present religious pluralism. The word 'unique' is itself ambiguous. A thing is unique when it has a distinctive character and is different from other comparable things. In this sense Christianity is unique, but so are the other religions. The word 'unique', however, can also mean that the thing in question is completely unlike all others and is superior to them; and this is probably what is meant when Christianity is said to be unique. In the climate of religious pluralism can this uniqueness be maintained?

In so far as we speak of religious pluralism and think of Christianity as one of the religions we have abandoned this second meaning of uniqueness. Earlier this century there were Christians who held that their religion was the only one that came from God, and that all the others were human constructions; and this made Christianity absolutely unique. Nowadays, however, many are moving towards the view that there is something of God in most, if not, all the religions, even if they cannot be said to come from him in the same way as Christianity. This view is becoming theologically respectable, and can be justified by a Christian criterion. In the Sermon on the Mount Jesus said that false prophets could be distinguished from true by their fruits. If we look impartially at the great world religions, we are bound to admit that they have produced many good fruits. They have been the basis of large, relatively stable communities, and have enabled millions of people to lead upright and meaningful lives. They may also have produced some bad fruits, but so also has Christianity, both in the past and at the present time; and so bad fruits, if not too many, do not cancel out good fruits. In so far, then, as religions have good fruits, God must have been working through them in some way or other.

From this one goes on to consider why there should be many religions. Here there is a fairly obvious reason, though it does not seem to have received much attention. In the world of about 5,000 years ago there were numerous small communities, each with its own language, and having relatively few contacts with other communities except its immediate neighbours. This isolation of language-based communities meant that each developed not merely its own language, but also the categories of thinking implicit in that language. We tend to think that what is stated in one language can be exactly translated into another language, but this is not so. In certain areas, of which religion is one, it is difficult to translate precisely between French and English because the terms employed in the two languages are not identical; for example, there is no good French word for 'fundamentalism' since the nearest word, *intégrisme* is not exactly the same. It is seldom realised that between Judaism and Christianity there is a difference in the meaning of the simple word 'day' (apart from its use for the period, of daylight); for a Western Christian a day consists of the period of twenty-four hours from midnight to midnight, but for a Jew a day is the period from sunset to sunset, and so is never exactly twenty-four hours.[4] Thus the Jewish Sabbath is not identical with the Christian Saturday, but begins on Friday at sunset. When we move on to more abstract ideas, the opportunities for divergence are even greater.

In my studies of early Islam I came to the conclusion that one of the factors underlying the rapid spread of the religion was the failure of the Christian Church to deal with the problem of cultural diversity. Three important groups had been declared heretics: the Copts of Egypt, the Syrian Jacobites and the Nestorians. By AD 600 the Church had come to be dominated by those from a Greek or Hellenistic cultural background. The ecumenical Christian creeds were formulated in terms of the current Hellenistic philosophy, and the Church was closely linked with Byzantine imperialism. I see the Copts, Jacobites and Nestorians as wanting to assert a cultural and ethnic identity distinct from that of the Greeks, and associated with their liturgical languages, Coptic, West Syriac and East Syriac. I have said something about this in the opening chapter of my book *Muslim–Christian Encounters* (and more briefly in *Testament*), and here will only add a simple illustration. In Greek culture the conception of the human being is dualistic, that is, he consists of soul and body, but it is the soul which is the essential person. What was thought about the body varied, but it was always secondary; at one extreme was the view expressed by the tag *sōma sēma*, 'the body is the tomb' (of the soul). The Copts, on the other hand, had a monistic view of the human person, which made the body as much part of it as the soul. This seems to be linked with the ancient Egyptian custom of mummifying the dead, which expresses a deep concern for the overcoming of bodily death. Egyptian Christians, even those like Athanasius not named as heretics, were above all anxious to ensure that each believer's body could become incorruptible through his sharing in the incorruptible body of Christ in the Eucharist. The point I want to make here is that these allegedly heretical views were attempts to express central truths of the Christian faith in terms of the distinctive cultures of the three groups.

In the diversity of cultures there are three features which are relevant to religion. Firstly, as has already been noted, the different categories of thinking associated with the various languages lead to different ways of understanding the world in which we live. Westerners now tend to think of evolution as occurring in many spheres besides biology, whereas Muslims think of the world and conditions in it as essentially unchanging. Secondly, communities have different views about what constitutes the great problem of life. The ancient Egyptians wanted above all to overcome bodily death; but in other communities the great problem is rather how to get enough to eat. Thirdly, in different communities the imaginative form of deep religious experiences will be different. The Old Testament prophets sometimes had visions and heard words being spoken to them; but Muhammad often seems merely to have found the words in his heart without seeing or hearing anything, though he believed the words had been brought to him by an angel. Because of these three culture-related features it is not surprising that religions should differ greatly from one another.

When one considers the diversity of cultures in the world in the second millennium BC and their relative isolation from one another, it is clear that during that period there was no possibility of one religion meeting the needs of all the cultural communities. There had to be a large number of religions, and each of these would normally grow out of the experiences of one or more individuals. In different regions in the course of time and for a variety of reasons several small communities became amalgamated in a larger one, and this would have a culture into which particular cultures had been fused. Some might even have disappeared almost completely. Such a process doubtless underlies the appearance of religions like Hinduism and Buddhism. These amalgamated cultures would, of course, differ greatly from one another. The later split in Christendom between Greek Orthodoxy and Roman Catholicism is largely due to the cultural difference between the regions of Latin culture and those of Greek culture. At the present day as Christianity spreads into Asia, Africa and Latin America, new forms of cultural diversity are appearing which require urgent attention, and they are not always receiving sympathetic treatment.

ii. The three aspects of God

In the world of today, the world of religious pluralism, it is becoming increasingly necessary that Christians should be able to give some defence of their belief in one God despite the fact that they worship Father, Son and Holy Spirit. This is especially so when they are in dialogue with Muslims, for these sometimes accuse Christians of worshipping three gods. To meet this challenge Christians need more help from theologians than they are getting at the moment, and something simpler than an exposition of the traditional Trinitarian doctrine of the ecumenical creeds. My feeling is that these formulations are too closely linked with a form of Hellenistic philosophy now outmoded, and that we require complementary formulations in terms of a modern post-Enlightenment philosophy; but this philosophy is still only emerging and has not taken proper shape. For the moment all I can do is to offer some suggestions to help people with their personal thinking.

The first thing to be said is that a modern English-speaking believer will make no progress in his thinking on this matter unless he banishes the word 'person' when speaking of one of the three. The reason for this is not that the doctrine has changed, but that the word 'person' has developed in meaning considerably since it was first used in English translations in the sixteenth century. The dominant connotation now is that of an individual human person, and, even if taken metaphorically, it is difficult to apply the word to the Godhead without introducing misleading suggestions. In the sixteenth century it was an acceptable translation of the Latin 'persona', which had first meant an actor's mask and then a role in a play. The idea of God having three roles is possible; and these could be defined as creator, redeemer and sanctifier. These indicate three areas where believers become aware of the activity of God in the world and in their own lives.

The traditional Greek formulation was one *ousia* (or essence) and three *hypostaseis* (or hypostasis); and there is something to be said for retaining 'hypostasis' just because we have no clear idea of what it means; we are indeed dealing with matters which we understand only imperfectly. In my own thinking I find it helpful to use the word 'aspect' which is not too far from the Greek *prosōpon* which was sometimes used in the discussions. There is nothing strange in one being having different aspects.

I also find it helpful to speak of the three aspects as the ontogenic aspect, the anthropic aspect and the energic aspect. These terms are not intended as an alternative formulation of Trinitarian doctrine, but only as an aid to discussion and personal thinking. I suggest 'ontogenic' for the first instead of the more obvious 'creative' in order to avoid the restriction of the divine activity to the initiation of the process (which 'creation' is often taken to mean), whereas it includes the communication of being to all humanity and indeed to all created beings. The anthropic aspect of God could be defined as that in God of which human beings are the image. It is also, of course, what is called 'the Word of God' and is involved in creation. The third aspect is the immanent action of God in human beings, calling, guiding and strengthening them. Perhaps along this line it may be possible for Christians to persuade their Muslim friends that they truly believe in God who is one and besides whom there is no deity.

iii. Moving into the future

The last two centuries have witnessed a great unification of the world through the greater speed and ease of travel and the improvement of all forms of communication between human beings. The process of unification will continue into the next century. The religious pluralism already mentioned is one result of it. Other results with which the various religions will have to deal are the emergence of a world intellectual outlook (primarily in non-religious matters) and the appearance of undesirable social trends. These two points need to be looked at separately.

By undesirable social trends I understand trends in our common life which are contrary to religious values, and these include the growth of secularism, consumerism and an undue emphasis on sexual pleasure. Secularism is to be seen in the increasing number of people in the West to whom God means little and who do not engage in any form of religious worship, while in the public political and economic life of Western communities slight attention is paid to religious beliefs and values. Consumerism is essentially an excessive reliance on material possessions, so that it becomes necessary to have all the latest gadgets, whether they are really necessary or not. It also includes the expectation of an ever higher standard of living and the demand for this; and it may often be combined with total disregard for the future of the world environment. Consumerism run riot is little better than greed, and is probably at the root of the conflicts which rage in many countries of the world.

Sex, again, has always been something of a problem for human beings, but recent developments have been particularly unfortunate. The root of the trouble here seems to be an exaggerated belief in the value of sexual pleasure, so that a life without lots of it is somehow imperfect and unsatisfactory. Such a belief is not usually clearly formulated but nevertheless it is all-pervasive, and is threatening the position of the family as the basis of a stable society.

These trends, secularism, consumerism and excessive sex, are contrary to the ethical principles of all the great religions. It should therefore be the aim of their leaders to establish some form of cooperation between them in order to counter the anti-religious influences. They should certainly, for example, have something to contribute towards a stronger and juster United Nations, which could control the powerful economic forces which are in danger of destroying our planet. They could perhaps also cooperate in encouraging their wealthier adherents to adopt a simpler lifestyle.

Another feature of the unification of the world is the way in which the Western intellectual outlook is coming to dominate the thinking of the whole human race, at least in its non-religious aspects. This outlook, of course, is far from monolithic, but there is a wide area in which it is possible to see something common. Science and the scientific view of the world have a central place, but historical methodology with its emphasis on objective historical fact is also important. For many Westerners, of course, Christian elements are included in their general outlook, but these have not greatly affected the non-Christian world. This Western intellectual outlook which is spreading throughout the world is thus religiously neutral, and so it is incumbent on the world religions to discover how their traditional thought-forms can somehow be combined with it.

The various religions also need to try to come to terms with one another through dialogue and in other ways. This means that each has to learn to appreciate the values of the others. Christians, for example, should be able to appreciate the Islamic emphasis on the transcendence of God without becoming Muslims; rather they are increasing the emphasis on something already present in their own tradition. It should be possible for the members of the various religions to progress a long way in appreciating the values of others without any question of a change of religious allegiance. Undoubtedly the unification of the world would seem to require a movement towards a single world religion, but that is not something for the foreseeable future; and in the present situation it is pointless to speculate on how one religion might be achieved.

My plan for helping non-Christians to appreciate the truths of Christianity would place more emphasis on history than on doctrine. At the centre would be an exposition of the humanity of Jesus. This would have to be preceded by a brief account of the Hebrew people's view of their place in history and of how God had acted on their behalf. Against this background the teaching and practice of Jesus, and his passion and crucifixion, could be presented as historical facts, and the non-Christians asked to try to understand his achievement against the background of their own tradition. When non-Christians accept the historical facts and try to interpret them for themselves, they will probably not, at least at first, accept the Christian belief in the divinity of Jesus. They may well, however, come to see that in these happenings there is something unique, and that Jesus did in fact achieve something of importance for the whole human race which has not been achieved by any adherent of another religion; and this would be to a great extent an admission of the uniqueness of Jesus. At the same time it is possible that what other religions have to say about Jesus might enable Christians to gain fuller insight into some aspects of the Gospel; and certainly Christians should always be ready to learn.

Many people are interested in interfaith dialogue and the possibilities of practical cooperation between religions; and all this I would certainly support.

Notes

1. A German philosopher who was awarded the Nobel Prize for Literature in 1908.
2. London, 1937.
3. Constance Evelyn Padwick (1886–1968) was a British missionary and writer.
4. See Genesis, Chapter 1.

6

William Montgomery Watt's Inaugural Lecture – Islamic Studies in Scotland: Retrospect and Prospect

University of Edinburgh
Inaugural Lecture, No. 27

Islamic Studies in Scotland: Retrospect and Prospect
W. Montgomery Watt
MA, PhD, BLitt
Professor of Arabic and Islamic Studies

The inauguration of the first Chair of Arabic and Islamic Studies in Scotland is an appropriate occasion for looking at the achievements of Scotsmen in this field in the past, and also for estimating the future prospects of such studies.

I shall presently show that Arabic studies by Scots are of some antiquity, and in a special sense may be said to be lost in the mists of legend; but we cannot claim any direct connection with Muhammad himself. There is, however, a source of confusion which threatens to turn Muhammad into a Scottish national hero, though probably not many in this audience are young enough to have been exposed to it. Writers of history textbooks for elementary schools have been ahead of many university departments of history in extending their purview far beyond Europe in remote centuries. Those of you who are parents may have heard eight-year-olds discoursing on the laws of Hamniurabi. The particular source of confusion which concerns us today is that, through an accident of chronology, the chapter in these textbooks on Columba at Iona tends to be followed by one on Muhammad and the origin of Islam. The following answer was actually given in an Edinburgh school a few years ago.[1]

> Mohammed was responsible for the spreading of Christianity in England. He had to flee from his native land, because the people did not believe him; and he took with him a Pope whose name was Gregory. They landed at a place now called Iona and he preached to the people there; and he then came to England to preach to the people there . . . and they took it in well.

Confusions aside, the first Scottish Arabist of note, Michael Scot, was active about the year 1200. Unfortunately he also dabbled, or was thought to dabble, in the black arts, and he came to have a great reputation as a sorcerer and magician, which gained him a place in Dante's *Inferno*. Sir Walter Scott made much use of the legend in *The Lay of the Last Minstrel*, and says of him: 'he cleft the Eildon hills in three, and bridled the Tweed with a curb of stone'. A less extravagant allegation, that he feasted his friends with dishes brought by spirits from the royal kitchens of France and Spain, has probably a simple nonmagical explanation. In the twelfth century Moorish Spain was far ahead of Western Europe in the arts of gracious living, not least gastronomy; and Michael Scot doubtless brought from Spain some new recipes, just as modern tourists might think of delighting their friends with gazpacho. The sober truth about Michael Scot is that he studied Arabic at Toledo, there met Arabic-speaking philosophers, Muslim and Jewish, and with some collaborators produced the first Latin translations of several works of Aristotle and of Arabic commentaries on these.[2]

Whether because of the danger of being implicated in the black arts, or for some more pedestrian reason, there was little Scottish interest in Arabic for several centuries. Perhaps Archbishop Laud, if Jenny Geddes had not flung that stool in protest at his liturgy, might have followed up his foundation of a Chair of Arabic at Oxford with another at Edinburgh. Just a little later than this – in 1649 – a Scotsman, Alexander Ross, became sufficiently interested in the Islamic religion to translate the Qur'an from French into English.[3] The suspicion of everything Islamic inherited from the war propaganda of the Crusading period was apparently still strong, for he thought it advisable to accompany his translation with an essay entitled 'A needful caveat or admonition for them who desire to know what use may be made of, or if there be danger in reading the Alcoran'. The opening words of this essay may be quoted:

> Good Reader, the great Arabian Imposter now at last after a thousand years, is by way of France arrived in England, and his Alcoran or Gallimaufry of Errors (a brat as deformed as the Parent, and as full of heresies as his scald-head was of scurffe) hath learned to speak English.[4]

It is possible that much of this was included chiefly in order to silence hostile critics. Ross thought quite highly of Muslims, and preceded Pierre Bayle, the author of the celebrated *Dictionary*, in using the merits of Islam as a foil to show up the weaknesses of contemporary Christianity.

> In reading the Alcoran, though we find much dung, yet in it we shall meet with some gold . . . in the dirt of the Alcoran you shall

find some Jewells of Christian vertues; and indeed if Christians will but diligently read and observe the Lawes and Histories of the Mahometans, they may blush to see how zealous they are in the works of Devotion, Piety and Charity, how devout, cleanly and reverend in their Mosques, how obedient to their Priests, that even the great Turk himself will attempt nothing without consulting his Mufti; how careful they are to observe their hours of prayers five times a day, wherever they are, and however imployed? . . . if we observe their justice, temperance and other moral! vertues, we may truly blush at our own coldness, both in devotion and charity, at our injustice, intemperance and oppression . . . and surely their devotion, piety and works of mercy are main causes of the growth of Mahometanisme, and on the contrary, our neglect of Religion, and looseness of conversation, is a main hindrance to the increase of Christianity . . .[5]

There are many reflections of a similar kind in a later book by the same author, especially when he discusses the reasons for the extension of Islam. This book is *Pansebeia, or a View of All the Religions of the World*. It is said to be the first work on comparative religion written in Europe, and was translated into German. One of the interesting points in it is that the author includes 'Mahumetanism' (as he calls it) along with Christianity under the heading of 'religions of Europe'. This is not surprising, of course, when we remember that the book was published in 1653 in the heyday of Ottoman power in central Europe.[6]

For about two centuries after the publication of *Pansebeia*, Scotsmen had little share in the slow development of Islamic studies among the scholars of the Christian West. During this period progress was indeed made in collecting accurate information about the history, manners and institutions of the Muslims, but a distorted 'image of Islam' and of the character of its founder had been inherited from medieval times, and this 'image' proved an incubus from which it was difficult to escape. Dean Humphrey Prideaux of Norwich in 1617 entitled a serious book on Muhammad *The True Nature of Imposture Fully Displayed in the Life of Mahomet*; and despite the erudite character of the work referred to its subject as 'the old lecher'. Not unexpectedly the judgement of a freethinker like Edward Gibbon was unfavourable, namely, that 'in his private conduct Mahomet indulged the appetites of a man and abused the claims of a prophet'. Such conceptions go back several centuries – as has been shown in detail in a book published a few years ago by our own university press[7] – to a period when Christendom felt itself threatened by Islam both militarily and spiritually. Islam was greatly feared, and in proportion the distorted image became deeply rooted in the outlook of Europeans, so that we are not yet completely free from it.

It was in correcting distortions that a great advance was made by Thomas Carlyle. He was not an Arabist nor an Islamist, but on 8 May 1840 in Edinburgh, as the second of his series 'On Heroes, Hero-worship and the Heroic in History', he delivered a lecture on Muhammad and Islam under the title of 'The Hero as Prophet'. He had read one or two of the chief scholarly books available in English and German; above all he had gone carefully through the excellent translation of the Qur'an by George Sale, trying to recreate for himself Muhammad's central religious experience, or rather experience of life. He did not find the Qur'an easy reading.[8]

> I must say, it is as toilsome reading as I ever undertook. A wearisome confused jumble, crude, incondite; endless iterations, long-windedness, entanglement; ... Nothing but a sense of duty could carry any European through the Koran. We read in it, as we might in the State-Paper Office, unreadable masses of

lumber, that perhaps we may get some glimpses of a remarkable man.

Yet this lecture is notable because Carlyle was the first man of repute in Europe to have the courage to say publicly and unequivocally that he believed Muhammad to be sincere. Men like Leibniz, Kant and Goethe had been prepared to allow that Islam was an expression of the one true religion; and Carlyle was doubtless influenced by Goethe on this point, for he refers to him twice in the lecture. His original contribution, however, was an imaginative reconstruction of the inner experience of Muhammad – 'this great fiery heart, seething, simmering, like a great furnace of thoughts'.

The reconstruction of Muhammad's experience was, of course, not in terms of the particular features of the Arabian background. In a sense 'Mahomet' was a peg for Carlyle's own ideas. Yet there was sufficient knowledge of detail to make it a valid protest against the denigration of Muhammad's character in the traditional image, and a genuine contribution to a more objective understanding of Muhammad and Islam. Thus he writes:

> He is by no means the truest of Prophets; but I do esteem him a true one. Farther, as there is no danger of our becoming, any of us, Mahometans, I mean to say all the good of him I justly can. It is the way to get at his secret . . .

Referring to a story that Muhammad had trained a pigeon to pick peas from his ear and then alleged that this was an angel dictating, Carlyle continued:

> It is really time to dismiss all that. The word this man spoke has been the life-guidance now of a hundred-and-eighty millions of men these twelve-hundred years . . . A greater number of God's creatures believe in Mahomet's word at this hour than in any other word whatever. Are we to suppose that it was a miserable

piece of spiritual legerdemain, this which so many creatures of the Almighty have lived by and died by? . . . I will believe most things sooner that that.

And a little later:

This Mahomet, then, we will in no wise ambitious schemer; we cannot conceive him so. The rude message he delivered was a real' one withal; an earnest confused voice from the unknown Deep . . . a fiery mass of Life cast-up from the great bosom of Nature herself.

This positive appreciation of Muhammad by Carlyle may be said to find an echo consider as an Inanity and Theatricality, a poor conscious in a positive appreciation of contemporary Muslims by one who had also seen the worst side of Islam, no less a figure than David Livingstone. He knew the depths of the evil of the slave trade and knew it mostly as the work of men called 'Arabs', whatever their precise racial character. Yet the last words in his diary, the words engraved on his monument in Westminster Abbey, are: 'All I can add in my solitude is may Heaven's rich blessing come down on every one, American, English or Turk, who will help to heal this open sore of the world.'

This is the older usage in which 'Turk' is roughly equal to 'Muslim'; and thus Livingstone has sufficient appreciation of the values of Islam to envisage the possibility of cooperation between Christians and Muslims *in* putting down slavery.[9]

From Livingstone it *is* natural to pass to the missionaries, many of whom have necessarily become competent in both Arabic and Islamics. Among such the names may be mentioned of John Hogg (1833–86),[10] William R. W. Gardner and Alexander Paterson (1863–1933?).[11] Hogg was 'a collier's wean' from East Lothian who did important work for the American Presbyterian Mission in Upper Egypt. The other two both made a beginning at Sheikh Othman (to be mentioned presently), and Paterson was later responsible for building a hospital at Hebron with which for a time in the 1940s I myself had some connection.

Two missionaries may be said to have passed the threshold of the academic world of Islamic scholarship, Temple Gairdner and Ion Keith-Falconer. The younger of these, Temple Gairdner (1873–1928), son of the Professor of Medicine at Glasgow and born at Ardrossan, devoted his life to missionary work in Cairo. A couple of books and an article in the German periodical *Der Islam* showed great promise; but the demands on his time made by administrative duties and his death at fifty-four prevented his scholarship from bearing much fruit. The excellence of the biography of him by Constance Padwick has been widely acclaimed.[12]

In many ways the most outstanding of the missionaries was the Honourable Ion Keith-Falconer (1856–87), third son of the Earl of Kintore. He was also the most colourful. While at school at Harrow he became interested in what was then called 'bicycling', and in his Cambridge days he was winner of many races, on one occasion defeating by a yard or two a gentleman styled 'the professional champion of the world'. Another feat was to ride from Land's End to John o'Groats in thirteen days – no mean feat in 1882, with poor roads and presumably a machine of the penny-farthing type without free-wheel. At Cambridge he read theology and then Semitic languages, but became more and more drawn to missionary work. Under the aegis of the Free Church of Scotland, though at his own expense, he prospected for a mission in South Arabia, and began to set up buildings at Sheikh Othman near Aden, but died from some obscure germ at the age of thirty-one. Before this, however, he had published one learned book and had been appointed to the Lord Almoner's Chair of Arabic at Cambridge. This chair – unfortunately later abolished – only required of its occupant that he should deliver *one* lecture in each academic year; and Keith-Falconer reckoned that, by choosing his dates carefully, he could if necessary spend a year and three-quarters continuously in South Arabia, and yet fulfil the obligations of his chair. This was distinctly better than our modern system of giving a man a sabbatical term, but perhaps the salary was commensurate with the amount of work. Many wives and others will appreciate a remark of Keith-Falconer's in a letter home from Aden, written at a time when he was teaching his wife Arabic: 'Arabic grammars should be strongly bound because learners are so often found to dash them frantically to the ground.'[13]

Ion Keith-Falconer forms a transition from missionaries to academics, and indeed is part of what one might call the Scottish period of Cambridge Arabic studies. In speaking of these matters my own loyalties are divided. I really belong, after Edinburgh, to 'the other place' – not to be interpreted eschatologically in an Islamic context – but it was at Cambridge that I was first initiated into the tongue of the angels, not at the University of Cambridge, however, but at the London School of Oriental and African Studies evacuated.

The first of these Cambridge professors is William Wright (1830–89). His father was a captain in the East India Company's service, and his mother a daughter of the last Dutch governor of Bengal. With the encouragement of his mother, herself a competent Orientalist, he specialised in Semitic languages at the University of St Andrews and continued his studies at Halle and Leipzig. After professorships at London and Dublin and other appointments he became Sir Thomas Adams' Professor of Arabic at Cambridge in 1870, and in his seventeen years' tenure of the chair – to quote a Cambridge panegyrist – 'lifted its fame to heights not hitherto approached'.[14] While he edited several Arabic texts of great importance at the time, he is chiefly remembered now for his Arabic grammar which is still the bane – or the joy – of many a student's life. The title page modestly says it is 'translated from the German of Caspari, with numerous additions and corrections', but in fact it is essentially his own work.[15] Once our students have recovered from the shock of plunging into these philological mysteries, I would recommend that they make a *ziyara* or 'pious visitation' of his grave beside the old Cathedral at St Andrews.

Wright was succeeded in his chair by another Scotsman, William Robertson Smith, who had previously held the other chair, the Lord Almoner's, for a short period. His career was brief but stormy. He was the son of a Free Church minister and himself trained for the ministry. For reasons which are obscure – but men were not specialised in those days – he spent two years as assistant in natural philosophy at Edinburgh before becoming Professor of Oriental Languages and Old Testament Exegesis in his old university of Aberdeen at the age of twenty-four. That was in 1870, but in 1881 he was removed from his chair because his views on certain Old Testament matters were regarded as heretical. London and Cambridge realised the stature of the scholar thus dismissed from Scotland, and he spent most of the rest of his life in the latter city – until his death in 1894 at the age of forty-eight. In the specifically Arabic field he is best remembered for his book on *Kinship and Marriage in Early Arabia* (1885) a pioneer work, based on Arabic sources, in what we now call social anthropology.

Students of Turkish have always been fewer in number than students of Arabic, and only one Scot has made a name for himself in this field. This is Elias John Wilkinson Gibb. He was born in Glasgow in 1857 and educated there. Through the *Thousand and One Nights* he came under the spell of the Orient, and at the age of twenty-five published a volume of *Ottoman Poems*. Before his early death in 1901, besides publishing other books, he had practically completed a six-volume *History of Ottoman Poetry* which combines sound scholarship with aesthetic appreciation.[16] By an irony of fate his name has become known, precisely because of his early death, far beyond the restricted circle of devotees of Ottoman Turkish poetry. His mother endowed an 'E. J. W. Gibb Memorial' which has published some fifty important works in the Arabic, Persian and Turkish fields, and still continues to function.

The nineteenth-century Scottish Arabist with the widest reputation was nowhere Professor of Arabic, but he reached an even higher academic level, because for eighteen years (1885–1903) he was Principal of this university. I refer to Sir William Muir. In the leisure of an Indian civil servant he began to write articles on the life of Muhammad which appeared first from 1855 on in the *Calcutta Review*, then grew to four volumes published in London in 1858–61. The work was subsequently revised by himself and then by T. H. Weir of Glasgow, and the last one-volume edition is still in print. Other works on Islamic history added to his reputation, and he also did what he could to advance the cause of Christian missions. As Principal of the University he seems to have ensured that the library took all the books on Islamic subjects being published in Europe, and he also left it his own Islamic and other books, constituting the Muir Collection. Some dozen years ago the university appropriately gave the name of William Muir Institute to the building housing the various oriental departments. As a personal reminiscence at second-hand – that is, with an *isnad* or transmission chain of only one link – I must mention how two or three people have described to me how it was the habit of Sir William Muir to ride up to the Old Quad on a white horse. While we can hardly expect our Principals nowadays to follow this example, it is a useful reminder of the place of the colourful and the dignified in university life.

Just after this period another Scotsman, Duncan Black Macdonald, became one of the world's leading Islamists. For many years he was professor at Hartford Seminary, Connecticut, editor of the quarterly called *The Moslem World*, and joint editor of a vast scholarly undertaking, *The Encyclopaedia of Islam*.

Latterly he had as collaborator in the *Encyclopaedia* the great French scholar Louis Massignon, who died three years ago, aged nearly eighty. I am happy to remember that in 1954 I was able to give Louis Massignon some practical information which facilitated his performance of an act of *pietas*, a pilgrimage to Macdonald's birthplace on a small island on the west coast of Scotland. In such an act one feels the spirit of the 'Auld Alliance' is still alive.

In the Scottish university tradition Arabic has of course been studied chiefly as an adjunct of Hebrew. Many of the professors of Hebrew have been competent Arabists, though without publishing much in the latter field. An exception, who deserves to be singled out for mention here, is William Barron Stevenson, for long professor in Glasgow, whose book *The Crusaders in the East* (1907), using Arabic sources, is still of value. He also wrote on 'Moslem Charms' – *not* those of the fair sex, of course, though he presented my department with an Egyptian lady's 'gear' for concealing or rather half-concealing her face. Arabic is now studied independently of Hebrew at Glasgow, St Andrews and Aberdeen.

Our own university of Edinburgh has had an independent lectureship in Arabic since 1912. Though the holders of the lectureship prior to myself are now dead, it so happens that one of those who taught Arabic here while it was in the Hebrew Department is still alive – indeed he guided my own first faltering steps, but not in 1911. This is Emeritus Professor Tritton of Aligarh and London, who is still hale and hearty.

The first of the independent lecturers was Edward Robertson who left Edinburgh in 1921 to take up a post in the British Museum. He was succeeded by Richard Bell, under whose supervision I myself had the good fortune to work. Bell might be said to follow in the Carlyle tradition, not merely in his desire to say all the good possible of Islam, but also because before his appointment he was minister of Wamphray which is next door to Carlyle's birthplace, so that he became a strong supporter of the Edinburgh Carlyle Society. By his studies in the Qur'an he made for himself an international reputation – but I hesitate to imagine what Carlyle would have said about his translation of that book. It was Richard Bell's aim to apply to the Qur'an the methods of higher criticism used for the Bible, and in particular to show how the short passages which were its original form had been modified and joined together to produce the text as we have it.

Parallel columns, dotted lines zigzagging across the page and other typographical devices, well justified academically, would have brought even stronger words from Thomas Carlyle than those he actually used. The translation is a careful, painstaking work which has not yet been fully digested by scholars and which will continue to be studied for many years to come. It was preceded by Gunning Lectures, published with the title *The Origin of Islam in its Christian Environment* (1926), and followed by the posthumous *Introduction to the Qur'an* (1953).

Richard Bell was a modest unassuming man, and probably few of his Edinburgh colleagues realised that in his own field he was one of the giants. The wives of scholars see these matters from a different angle. I remember Mrs Bell speaking with great feeling of 'those ten terrible years' when her husband was buried in his translation work. But this is a complaint which echoes through the centuries. An eighth-century Muslim savant, when he was at home, used to arrange his books round him and become so absorbed in them that he was oblivious of all worldly concerns. He had only one wife, where as a Muslim he might legally have had four, but this poor woman has been remembered for 1,200 years as having remarked, 'These books! – they are worse for me than three other wives would have been.'¹⁷

One further fact about Edinburgh may be briefly noted. The doyen of Islamic studies in the English-speaking world, Sir Hamilton Gibb of London, Oxford and Harvard, began his study of Arabic here, and is both a graduate and an honorary graduate of our university.

So much for the past. For the rest of this lecture I propose to turn to the present and future. What of Arabic and Islamic studies today and for the rest of this century? In this age of jet aircraft we are as far from Sir William Muir's white horse as he was from Michael Scot's wizardry; and the academic implications of jet aircraft are only beginning to be appreciated. Already before 1938 experts *in* foreign affairs and military matters realised that it was a strategic necessity to have in the country far more persons than we then had with a good knowledge of Asian and African languages. The Scarbrough Commission was appointed, and its report led to an expansion of oriental studies throughout Britain after the war. As part of this expansion Edinburgh added Persian, Turkish and for a time Urdu to the languages taught, and also enlarged the Department of Arabic and Islamic Studies, among other things adding a degree course in Islamic History.

A second phase of expansion was initiated by the report of the Hayter Commission in 1961. In this phase the chief development at Edinburgh so far has been the creation of a Centre of African Studies. My department is one of those cooperating in this centre, and this link promises to be of increasing importance. Apart from North Africa (Egypt to Morocco), which is solidly Muslim and Arabic-speaking, Arabic has been widely used in East and West Africa. In West Africa it is now known that there are several thousand uncatalogued Arabic manuscripts and documents. The religion of Islam is expanding in sub-Saharan Africa at a much faster rate than Christianity. A year or two ago something like two-thirds of the heads of independent states in Africa were Muslims. By the end of the century it is likely that Islam will be the dominant religion of Africa: and, partly because of this, it is in Africa that the most interesting developments within Islam are to be expected during the next few decades. For such reasons the connection of the Arabic Department with the Centre of African Studies is likely to be increasingly fruitful.

Let us, however, go back to the academic implications of jet aircraft – other than the production of a race of 'globe-trotting dons'. The 'jet' is a symbol of the greater ease of communications throughout the planet. In the 1920s it was an adventure for a student to go to Germany, but nowadays anything this side of Yugoslavia is commonplace. The number of overseas students in Britain is constantly increasing, and likewise the number of non-European settlers from various parts of the Commonwealth. Exchanges of academic staff have become the order of the day. There is also greater readiness among ordinary people to spend some years in a foreign country.

It is important to see these facts in perspective. Up to 1940 it is roughly true that the world existed in several separate cultural compartments. The main ones – if we follow Arnold Toynbee's analysis – were the Western (our own), the Orthodox Christian (south-east Europe and Russia), the Hindu, the Far Eastern and the Islamic (stretching from West Africa through the Middle East to Malaysia and Indonesia).

There were regions where two cultures overlapped; but on the whole the contacts between cultures were limited, and each preserved its own identity. The chief exception is that Western or Euramerican culture has for some centuries, and especially since 1800, been expanding into the other culture areas. Its science and technology are being universally adopted, though its ideas and values have not won the same degree of acceptance. With the decline of Western imperialism and colonialism and the emergence of many independent states the ancient cultures have been striving to reaffirm their identity in this technological world.

Thus in this age of jet aircraft there are two complementary features relevant to the present argument – a greater mixing or people from different cultural backgrounds, and a recovery of a sense of self-identity by the older cultures of the Middle East and Asia, perhaps even of an awareness that they have a mission to the rest of the world. Though our science and technology pervade the planet, their development has perhaps only been achieved at the cost of the atrophy of other faculties. There is little justification for holding that in all respects other than science and technology our culture is superior. Just as all states are on an equal footing in the United Nations, so there is an equality in the cultural field in the sense that we have to approach as equals those from other cultural backgrounds and humbly to recognise that we ourselves may have something to learn from those we used to call 'lesser breeds without the law'.

These points are doubtless familiar to you, but we are only beginning to realise that they have academic implications. The motives for the appointment of the Scarbrough and Hayter commissions were chiefly practical and utilitarian, and the growth of student interest in languages like Russian and Chinese is presumably due to the realisation that these languages will be of great practical importance in the future. Yet there is another aspect which must not be forgotten. If we are to live in a world where men from different cultures are meeting on a basis of equality, is it satisfactory to have an ideal of education which restricts itself to Western or Euramerican culture? Journalists and news commentators indeed contrive to give even the average man some idea of the background of current events in Asia and Africa; but a university must surely look beyond this and envisage some deeper study of non-European cultures.

Such study, too, can no longer be left to a few enthusiasts or eccentrics, but must be widely spread among university graduates.

It seems probable that by the year 2000 no man will be considered truly educated unless he has engaged at university level in some study of a non-European culture. It is the special function of the departments dealing with the languages and cultures of Asia and Africa to provide the educated man of the 'jet' age with some more profound appreciation of those cultures. Perhaps we should look forward to the time when the greatest works of Islamic and other Asian cultures are read and respected along with those of Greece and Rome as 'classics' of the 'one world'. This extended conception of the 'Classics' might well affect school education.

Already for practical reasons some of the difficult oriental languages are being taught in school.

One English school has classes in Chinese, while several dozen high schools in the eastern United States teach Arabic. What I have just said, however, shows that there are good educational reasons for such a development. So I would like here, after this review of the extensive Scottish share in Islamic studies, to commend to our headmasters and headmistresses the possibility of introducing Arabic (or Chinese or Sanskrit) in schools. As a language Arabic is easier than Chinese; its grammar, despite Ion Keith-Falconer's remark, has fewer exceptions than French; its writing is no more difficult than shorthand; only its vocabulary is vast.

Arabic at school would be not just practically useful but a contribution to education in the deepest sense.

Finally, I would like to express my personal thanks to the university for the creation of this chair, and I would also give voice to the hope that Scotland may play a worthy part in the continuing work of bringing Europeans and Americans to a deeper appreciation of the values of Islamic culture.

Notes

1. This was communicated to the author by Professor James Barr.
2. Cf. Bernard Lewis, *British Contributions to Arabic Studies*, London. 1941, 10. Cf. also *Encyclopaedia Britannica* (1962 edition). A traveller who went beyond using recipes was John, Fourth Marquis of Bute, who compiled a small volume of Moorish Recipes, privately printed (posthumously) about 1952 in Edinburgh.
3. Sieur du Ryer, *The Alcoran of Mahomet: Translated out of Arabique into French*, London, 1649.
4. Ibid., p. 406.
5. Ibid., 413 f.
6. In the fourth edition, London, 1672, the section on Islam is pp. 162–79. Cf. also Gustav Pfannmüller, *Handbuch der Islam-Literatur*, Berlin, 1923, 157, 161, 164, 170.
7. Norman Daniel, *Islam and the West: the Making of an Image*, Edinburgh, 1960.
8. The quotations are taken from 'The shilling edition' of Carlyle's works, London, 1890.
9. Quoted from Kenneth Cragg, *The Dome and the Rock*, London, 1964, 290.
10. Biography by Rena L. Hogg, *A Master-builder on the Nile*, Pittsburgh, 1914.
11. Biography by William Ewing, *Paterson of Hebron*, London, n.d.
12. Constance Padwick, *Temple Gairdner of Cairo*, London, 1929.
13. Robert Sinker, *Memorials of the Hon. Ion Keith-Falconer*, London, 1888; the last quotation is on p. 156 of the third edition, 1903.
14. A. J. Arberry, *The Cambridge School of Arabic*, Cambridge, 1948, 25.
15. Ibid., 30.
16. *Journal of the Royal Asiatic Society*, 1902, 486–9.
17. Ibn Khallikan, tr. de Slane, ii, 582, of the wife of az-Zuhri (d. 742).

PART 3

REFLECTIONS ON THE WORK OF WILLIAM MONTGOMERY WATT

7

Scottish Pioneers of Arabic and Islamic Studies: Reflections on Selected Parts of the Inaugural Lecture of Professor Watt, Given in Edinburgh in October 1965

David Kerr[1]

Introduction

William Montgomery Watt was elevated to the Chair of Arabic and Islamic Studies at the University of Edinburgh in 1964. In addition to marking a distinguished personal achievement for Professor Watt, the occasion was an important moment in the history of the university, and of Scotland itself. It was the first time that a professorship was recognised in this field in any Scottish university. Although Edinburgh, like other ancient universities in Scotland, had a tradition of including some Arabic in the curricula of Semitic languages, and had created a dedicated lectureship in Arabic and Islamic studies in 1912 – to which Montgomery Watt was appointed in 1947 – there had never before been a professor in this field in Scotland. Yet the intellectual history of Scotland had produced a remarkable number of scholars with interests in Islam. It was fitting therefore that Professor Watt devoted his inaugural lecture, given in October 1965, to reviewing of the genesis and the evolution of this field of scholarship in Scotland, under the title 'Islamic Studies in Scotland: Retrospect and Prospect'.

An Analysis of the Contribution of Scottish Scholars to Arabic and Islamic Studies Discussed in Professor Watt's Inaugural Lecture

Seventeenth-century origins: Alexander Ross

Scottish interests in Islam go back as far as the mid-seventeenth century when Alexander Ross published the first English translation of the Qur'an (1649) – though he worked from an existing French translation rather than the original Arabic. If Ross's work as translator was less than original, it aroused a personal esteem for much that he discovered in Islamic scripture, and it prompted him to write about Islam with insights that were unusual for his day. In gentle rebuke of Christian polemic against Islam he commented in the introduction to his translation:

> If Christians will but diligently read and observe the Lawes and Histories of the Mahometans, they may blush to see how zealous they are in the works of Devotion, Piety and Charity . . . If we observe their justice, temperance and other morall virtues, we may truly blush at our own coldnesse.

Ross developed his comparative approach in a second work entitled *Pansebeia, or a View of All the Religions of the World* (1653). Reflecting the impact of the Ottoman Empire in the Balkans, he included Islam among the religions of Europe. He emphasised the proximity of Islam to Christianity in terms of origin, teaching and place, and suggested that Christianity might regenerate its own strengths by emulating those of Islam. Quoting Ross at the beginning of his lecture, Professor Watt set the direction and tone of all that followed: 'I would give voice to the hope that Scotland may play a worthy part in the continuing work of bringing Europeans and Americans to a deeper appreciation of the values of Islamic culture.'

If Professor Watt's citations of Alexander Ross suggest the combination of mind and heart that inspired his own interests in Islam, his intellectual bearings were more deeply rooted in Scottish contributions to the evolution of Arabic and Islamic studies in the second half of the nineteenth century and the first half of the twentieth. Like great actors, these scholars stride the stage of Professor Watt's lecture, whilst he, as both dramatist and critic, gives each their voice, and evaluates each in the evolution of the drama as a whole.

Nineteenth-century polarities: Thomas Carlyle and William Muir

Pride of place is given to Thomas Carlyle (d. 1881), the Scottish philosopher and essayist of the mid-nineteenth century, who – though not a scholar of either Arabic or Islam – was, in Professor Watt's esteem: 'the first man in Europe to have the courage to say publicly and unequivocally that he believed Muhammad to be sincere'.

The occasion was the lecture that Carlyle gave in his celebrated series entitled 'On Heroes, Hero-worship, and the Heroic in History'. In the second of these lectures he took 'Mahomet' as 'The Hero as Prophet' and proceeded 'to say all the good of him I justly can'. Modesty matching the moment, Professor Watt made no reference to his own writings: either to his two studies of *Muhammad at Mecca* and *Muhammad at Medina* that include several references to Carlyle, or to the article he published on 'Carlyle on Muhammad' in *The Hibbert Journal* in 1954. It was in the article that he gave his most reasoned appreciation of Carlyle.

In sharp relief to the sullen history of Christendom's antipathy toward Islam, Carlyle's originality lay in acknowledging that

Muhammad was patently sincere, and that he personified qualities of prophethood that elucidate the very essence of 'the hero as prophet': he lived in harmony with nature as the 'clothing' of God's universal presence; he transformed human apprehensions of reality, and inspired others to make these heroic qualities their own; he reshaped human history and built a new movement of civilisation. Carlyle's portrait of Muhammad may indeed have been 'a peg for his own ideas', as Professor Watt put it in his lecture, but in terms of the history of Christian antipathy toward Islam, it marked a moment of transition: 'It is an important step forward in the process of reversing the medieval world-picture of Islam as the great enemy, and of rehabilitating its founder, Muhammad.'

Echoing Carlyle, Professor Watt commented: 'The Muslims are our neighbours in the "one world", and it is incumbent upon us, if we are to be good neighbours, to learn to say all the good of them we justly can.'

Carlyle was less concerned with the state of Christian–Muslim relations than with criticising nineteenth-century Christianity that he perceived to be succumbing to scepticism, materialism and apathy. He lambasted: 'mechanistic religion – turgid dogmas, empty practices, and gaudy vestments, all signs of "mumbling delirium prior to dissolution"'. To save religion from such decline, he turned to German romanticism. In Goethe he discovered the appreciation of 'Islam' as 'submission' to God. To Goethe's question: 'If this be Islam, do we not all live in Islam?', Carlyle replied:

> Yes, all of us that have any moral life, we all live so. It has ever been held the highest wisdom of man not merely to submit ... (but) to cease his frantic pretension of scanning this great God's-World in his small fraction of a brain; to know that it has verily, though deep beyond his soundings, a Just Law, that the soul of it was Good.

With this larger question of the nature of religion Professor Watt was himself deeply concerned. The year before his appointment to the Chair of Arabic and Islamic Studies, he published his first extended inquiry into the nature of religion and the relationship among religions in his *Truth in the Religions: a Sociological and Psychological Approach*. Here he explores the elements that comprise 'religious ideation' – that is, all that empowers religion with moral and spiritual dynamism. Distinguishing a prophet from a poet or mystic, he defined a prophet's teaching as: 'an ideational synthesis, including dynamic ideas in projection, that express some essential features of the world in which the prophet and his contemporaries have to live'.

The correspondence with Carlyle's philosophy of religion is striking and it is the clue to what Professor Watt had in mind when referring, in his inaugural lecture, to 'the Carlyle tradition'. Carlyle had his own connections with Edinburgh. He is said to have walked to the city from his Border village of Ecclefechan to begin his studies in divinity, and later – when he lost his childhood faith – in philosophy. He later served as University Rector (1866).

Richard Bell – Montgomery Watt's predecessor as Lecturer in Arabic and Islamic Studies, and his esteemed teacher – was an admirer of Carlyle. Bell's career began as a Church of Scotland minister in Wamphray, next to Ecclefechan, and as university lecturer he became a leading figure in the Edinburgh Carlyle Society. His own writing on Islam quoted Carlyle's lecture on Muhammad with approval: 'He laughed out of court the idea of an imposter being the founder of one of the world's great religions.'

It was Bell who introduced Montgomery Watt to Carlyle and who invited him to address the Society on Carlyle's view of Muhammad. In paying respect to Richard Bell in the inaugural lecture, Professor Watt clearly intended to associate his chair with 'the Carlyle tradition' in which they both stood.

Carlyle, however, was not the only Edinburgh luminary to lay intellectual foundations for an approach to Islam. As Professor Watt's lecture went on to note, 'the nineteenth-century Scottish Arabist with the widest reputation' was Sir William Muir, Principal of the University for eighteen years (1885–1903). Muir mastered Arabic, and also Persian and Urdu, in his earlier career in the Indian Civil Service, in which he rose to the rank of Lieutenant-Governor of the North-West Provinces. As a leisure-time pursuit he collected Arabic manuscripts, on the basis of which he wrote several works on Islamic history and religion, the centrepiece of his scholarship being a four-volume study of *The Life of Mahomet*. Originating as a series of articles in the *Calcutta Review*, the work was subsequently enlarged and published in London between 1858 and 1861. In its time, it was critically acclaimed as the foremost study of its kind in the English language, rivalling the other major European source for the life of Muhammad in Aloys Sprenger's *The Life of Muhammad*, first published in Allahabad in 1851, and in augmented form in German, entitled *Das Leben und die Lehre des Mohammad*.

Muir was unquestionably more learned about Muhammad's life than was Carlyle. *The Life of Mahomet* drew extensively on early Arabic sources, and presents a full account of the Prophet's career. Nor was Muir lacking in a sense of historical criticism, questioning the historical value of the *hadith* literature on account of its excessive piety, and preferring earlier to later biographical sources. Carlyle's essay, preceding both Sprenger's and Muir's work, was blithely disinterested in such technical questions. Carlyle knew nothing of the distinction that Muir was to draw between the two phases of Muhammad's career: in Mecca where Muir conceded that Muhammad gave every appearance of being a prophet, believing that he 'spoke literally in the name of God'; and in Medina where Muir detected a 'rapid moral declension', intolerance replacing persuasion in Muhammad's style of leadership.

The more interesting contrast between Muir and Carlyle, however, lay in their respective interpretations of Muhammad. If Carlyle, like Goethe, was determined to find as much good in Islam as was possible on the basis of his slender knowledge, Muir suborned his extensive learning to his commitment, as a senior figure in the Indian Civil Service, to disseminating 'English' culture, and with it Christianity. Criticising the pre-Raj attitudes of the East India Company, he bemoaned: 'England was then sadly neglectful of her responsibility; her religion was shown only at home, and she was careless of the spiritual darkness of her benighted subjects abroad.'

He devoted his years of colonial service to what he termed the 'enlightenment of India', by which he meant its Anglicisation and Christianisation. Islam, he argued in his historical writings, retarded the growth of civilisation among Muslim peoples: 'The Moslem faith, unlike the Christian, is powerless to adapt ... We fail of finding anywhere the germ of popular government or approach to free and liberal institutions.'

Muir's moral judgement was already evident in his earliest publication entitled *The Muhammadan Controversy* that appeared in the *Calcutta Review* in 1845. The title alluded to the epic confrontation between a German pietist missionary, Carl Pfander – working in India under the aegis of the English Church Missionary Society – and leading Indian Muslim religious scholars in Agra. Pfander's performance was found wanting in its grasp of issues of scholarship, both Christian and Islamic, and Muir resolved to redress the latter in *The Muhammadan Controversy*. His study of Muhammad flowed from this original excursus into religious polemics and reflected his theological as much as his historical convictions. His Christian identity was founded on the dogmatic certainty of the Presbyterian Westminster Confession, with its insistence that those who do not profess the Christian religion cannot be saved, 'be they ever so diligent to frame their lives according to the light of nature and the law of that religion they do possess'.

Carlyle's *The Hero and Prophet* and Muir's *Muhammadan Controversy* appeared within five years of each other. Their difference of religious perspective could scarcely have been sharper. Carlyle's Muhammad was instinctively attuned to nature as 'the clothing of God', while Muir's was corrupted by a lust for nature that resulted in his 'moral declension'. Professor Watt did not explore this contrast in his lecture, and his only comment on Muir was that 'he did what he could to advance the cause of Christian missions.'

The Cambridge Scots: William Wright, William Robertson Smith and E. J. W. Gibb

It is illuminating to consider the significance Watt attached to another line of Scottish contribution to the study of Middle Eastern languages and cultures in what he termed 'the Scottish period of Cambridge Arabic studies'. This refers to the second half of the nineteenth century when three Scottish scholars dominated the field of Islamic studies in England: William Wright (d. 1889), William Robertson Smith (d. 1894), and Elias John Wilkinson Gibb (d. 1901). They pioneered and together straddled the Orientalism of the late nineteenth century.

William Wright was a philologist. Born in Bengal, he was steeped in languages of Asia before returning to Europe – Scotland, Germany and the Netherlands – for his university education in Semitic languages. His expertise lay in Syriac and Arabic, and thus in comparative Semitic languages. In addition to his various editions and translations of Syriac and Arabic texts, his monumental *A Grammar of the Arabic Language* secured his place in the history of European scholarship of Semitic tongues. This two-volume work was based on two European precedents: Carl Paul Caspari's

Grammatica Arabica that was published in German between 1844 and 1888, and Silvestre de Sacy's *Grammaire Arabe* of 1810. Both these predecessors organised their presentation of Arabic grammar on the system of medieval Arab grammarians themselves, rather than attempting to fit Arabic into Latin grammatical forms. Both Caspari and de Sacy were interested in the metaphysics of language, especially the Cartesian idea that grammatical structures of individual languages display elements that are common to all. Like his predecessors, Wright wanted to produce more than a technical guide to the Arabic language – whether 'the bane – or the joy – of many a student's life', as Professor Watt quipped; Wright aspired to construct the linguistic bridge between English and Arabic that would contribute to metaphysical understanding among English- and Arabic-speaking cultures. Wright held the Sir Thomas Adams' Chair of Arabic at the University of Cambridge for nearly twenty years. Among his publications were his *Lectures on Comparative Grammar of Semitic Languages* that he gave with another Scot, William Robertson Smith.

More than thirty years younger than Wright, Robertson Smith arrived in Cambridge as an intellectual refugee from his home city of Aberdeen. Reputedly the most brilliant student of his generation in Scotland, he was appointed Professor of Oriental Languages and Old Testament in Aberdeen in 1870 at the age of twenty-four, having graduated in Divinity from Edinburgh. He held the chair for a decade during which he emerged as the Scottish pioneer of higher criticism of the biblical text. This provoked the ire of the Free Church, of which he was a minister; he was censured for heresy by the Free Church Assembly, and was removed from his chair. To escape the fury of Presbyterianism he moved south in 1881, and spent the remainder of his life in Cambridge – where the requirement of religious orthodoxy for professors had been lifted in 1871. In consultation with William Wright, and eventually as his successor in the Chair of Arabic, Robertson Smith advanced his studies in the interaction of philology, history, social anthropology and biblical studies. In terms of Arabic studies his most influential works were *Kinship and Marriage in Early Arabia* and the *Lectures on the Religion of the Semites*, both of which commanded attention among religionists, anthropologists and historians through the early decades of the twentieth century. Combined with his biblical scholarship, these gave him a deep insight into the nature of the religious scholarship, or scholarship of religion. Repudiating the hegemony of dogmatic theology, he argued for the integration of the intellect and the heart in exploring the ethical wealth of religions. He wrote that:

> there should be no discordance between the religious and the scholarly methods of study. They lead to the same goal. The more closely our study fulfils the demands of historical scholarship, the more fully it corresponds with religious needs.

Elias John Wilkinson Gibb's short life began in Glasgow where he was born and educated in the mid-nineteenth century, the son of wealthy Glasgow merchants of ancient Scottish ancestry. Glasgow at this time was the second largest city of the British Empire, and it was here that the Orient captivated the imagination of the young Glaswegian. Gibb was fascinated by the Ottoman Empire, and he turned his attention to the study of Ottoman Turkish and its legacy of poetry, traditionally the most important mode of expression of Ottoman intellectual thought. By the age of twenty-five he published his first collection of *Ottoman Poems*, and in Cambridge he went on to prepare a six-volume study entitled *A History of Ottoman Poetry*. This was the first comprehensive study of Ottoman literature, the selected poets being placed in their historical and literary contexts, with versified English translations of excerpts of their work. The other six volumes were published in 1900, and the following year Gibb died at the age of forty-one. His reputation was secured as the first major British scholar of Ottoman Turkish civilisation, and his name lived on also in the E. J. W. Gibb Memorial Trust, founded and financed by his family. Dedicated to the advancement of knowledge, especially through the editing and translation of Arabic, Persian and Turkish texts, the Gibb Memorial Trust stimulated the development of twentieth-century Islamic studies by making key works of Islamic culture accessible to English-language scholarship.

Professor Watt was never himself a Cambridge student, though he spent three years as a regular commuter to the city when taking Arabic courses through the School of Oriental Studies that was evacuated from London during World War II. He learned much, however, from the remarkable breadth of Scottish Oriental scholarship in late nineteenth-century Cambridge, and in his own career in scholarship he emulated its combination of linguistic, social and textual studies. One is struck particularly by the correspondence between William Robertson Smith's vision, and that which was to characterise Watt's own career and writings. Their life circumstances were quite different, and Professor Watt never had to endure the moral censure that drove Robertson Smith from Scotland. But their intellectual journeys led them to similar destinations, especially regarding the matrix of history, culture and religion. If Professor Watt was to broaden the relationship between religious and secular disciplines to include science, sociology and psychology as well as history and anthropology, his inclusive approach to Arabic and Islamic scholarship built on the foundations laid by Professor Robertson Smith half a century earlier.

Religious scholarship: Ion Keith-Falconer, William Temple Gairdner, Duncan Black Macdonald

Returning to the categories of Scots who contributed to Arabic and Islamic studies, Professor Watt's inaugural lecture acknowledged the role that Christian mission played in nineteenth- and early twentieth-century Scottish history. David Livingstone led the way, and, inspired by his heroism, many others followed. The first World Missionary Conference that convened in Edinburgh in 1910 recognised Scotland's missionary tradition:

> In the earlier missionary enterprise which evangelised Europe no country was more prominent than Scotland, and no country has in proportion to its size contributed to the evangelisation of the world during the last century so large a number of distinguished and devoted missionaries.

Several Scots were prominent in mission among Muslims. Livingstone himself formed alliances with African Muslims in the struggle against the East African slave trade. Professor Watt alluded to this by reminding his audience of the words engraved on Livingstone's memorial in Westminster Abbey: 'All I can add in my solitude is "May Heaven's rich blessing come down on every one, American, English or Turk, who will help to heal this open sore of the world".'

John Hogg (d. 1886) is also mentioned as the first Scottish missionary to become a competent Arabist during his years of service in Egypt. True to his lecture's theme, however, Professor Watt focused on Scottish missionaries who 'may be said to have passed the threshold of the academic world of Islamic scholarship'. These were Ion Keith-Falconer (d. 1887) and William Temple Gairdner (d. 1928), two colourful characters who contributed both to Christian mission and to Arabic and Islamic scholarship. The former was a hero of Scottish mission, second only to Livingstone himself. Athletic, academic and aristocratic, son of the Laird of Kintore on the Aberdeenshire Don, he entered the University of Cambridge to study mathematics, then divinity, before specialising in oriental languages – Hebrew, Syriac and Arabic. A brief visit to Egypt to study colloquial Arabic with John Hogg led him to discover his double vocation – for scholarship and mission. Back in Cambridge he translated and published the famous *Fables of Bidpai*, known in Arabic as *Khalila wa Dimna*, using both the Syriac and Arabic texts, he began lecturing on Hebrew, and in 1886 was elevated to the Lord Almoner's Professorship in Arabic. Since this involved but one lecture a year, he was able to combine it with creating a Christian mission in Aden, sponsored by the Free Church of Scotland and paid for by his family fortune. He arrived in Aden in December 1886, and died of fever in May 1887.

Assessments of Keith-Falconer's short career vary, but Professor Watt seems to have admired the precedent he set for an intellectual engagement with Islam, founded upon sound scholarship and the desire for human relationship with Muslims. It was this same combination of aspirations that first embarked Montgomery Watt on his venture with Islam, under the auspices of the Jerusalem and the East Mission of the Anglican Church. His sojourn in Jerusalem was short and disappointing in terms of intellectual engagement with Islam. Although he never resumed active association with the institutional side of Christian mission, and was indeed sharply critical of it, he maintained a lively interest in the issue of mission itself, regarding which he was develop some rather original views. While it is fruitless to speculate how Keith-Falconer may have developed had he lived, it is intriguing that Professor Watt spoke warmly of him in his lecture, and one might not be mistaken in concluding that in Ion Keith-Falconer he found a light for his own course, a forerunner in the 'transition from missionaries to academics'.

If William Temple Gairdner's career was less dashing than Keith-Falconer's, it was no less dramatic in terms of the interaction of missionary and scholarly concerns; and although his life was also cut short at the height of its power, he left a more substantial literary legacy that Keith-Falconer, and had a more definite impact on Protestant thinking about Islam in the early twentieth century. Born and educated in Glasgow, he went on to the University of Oxford from where he joined the Church Missionary Society and spent the rest of his life in Egypt. There he patiently mastered Arabic, a language that he used for scholarship as well as communication, and also for his own compositions in drama and hymnody. He returned to Scotland to participate in the Edinburgh World Missionary Conference (1910), of which he wrote the semi-official conference report, and then went on to North America to study with another Glaswegian, Duncan Black Macdonald, at the Hartford Seminary Foundation. Macdonald studied Arabic in Leipzig, and his subsequent appointment as Professor of Arabic and Islamic Studies in Hartford was itself a historic occasion: for his was the first such professorship to be created in the United States, and its remit included the intellectual formation of missionaries working in 'Muslim lands'. Under Macdonald's supervision, Gairdner prepared a translation and commentary on one of the great mystical texts of Islam, al-Ghazali's *Mishkat al-anwar*, '*The Niche of Lights*', that explores the Qur'anic metaphor of God as Light. He later recalled this scholarly task as amounting to a personal 'conversion', leading him to abandon the negativity toward Islam that had originally impelled his missionary vocation, and to adopt instead an irenic approach based on his belief that the Spirit of God could be truly discerned in the work of al-Ghazali, and in the lives of pious Muslims. The changing title of another book that he wrote during this period reflects the conversion: first published under the title *The Reproach of Islam* (1909), which laid the onus on Christian criticism of Islam, later revised editions appeared under the title *The Rebuke of Islam* to reflect his sensitivity to ways in which Islamic piety rebuked Christian neglect. His final essay, *The Value of Christianity and Islam*, espoused the dominant theological mood of the 1910 Edinburgh Conference which saw the Gospel as the fulfilment of other religions, and developed the idea of Islam as a *praeparatio evangelica*.

The brevity of Professor Watt's treatment of Gairdner in his lecture, while not in the least disrespectful of his scholarship, may convey a discomfort with his theological construction of Christianity's relationship with Islam. He was, by contrast, quite appreciative of Duncan Black Macdonald, rating him as 'one of the world's leading Islamists'. In addition to supervising missionary research, Macdonald produced several major scholarly works, of which the most important were his *Development of Muslim Theology, Jurisprudence and Constitutional Theory* and *The Religious Attitude and Life in Islam*. He was also a joint editor of the massive *Encyclopedia of Islam* on which he collaborated with, among others, the leading French scholar, Louis Massignon. The two men shared an affinity for mysticism, both in their scholarly interests and personal lives. Both sought through their studies of Sufism to seed a love of Islam in the hearts of Christians, and to cultivate a spiritual friendship that transcended while yet respecting doctrinal differences. Massignon regarded Macdonald as a saintly figure, and he visited his birthplace in Scotland and his grave in Connecticut. Professor Watt recalled how he had been 'able to give Louis Massignon some practical information which facilitated his performance of an act of pietas, a pilgrimage to Macdonald's birthplace on a small island on the west coast of Scotland'.

For both Macdonald and Massignon, scholarship of Islam was an exercise of 'religious scholarship', by which they meant the very antithesis of what 'religious studies' has later come to denote. Far from prescinding the issue of faith, their explorations of Islam could be termed 'adventures of faith'. For the most part unstated, and never degenerating into off-the-cuff romanticism, their spiritual engagement with Islam served to combine their scholarship with empathy that eschewed the polemical intent of most medieval scholarship. In his own writings on Islam Professor Watt was reticent about things spiritual, but he shared with Macdonald, Gairdner and Massignon a desire to integrate the intellect and spirit in a holistic approach to the study of religion.

The foundation of modern Islamic studies in Edinburgh: Richard Bell

This holistic approach was incipient in the early twentieth-century growth of Arabic and Islamic studies in Edinburgh. It was firmly grounded in textual and historical studies. The first steps were taken while Arabic was still under the aegis of Hebraic studies. Arthur Tritton was the lecturer, and although it was as a professor in the Aligarh University and the School of Oriental Studies in London that he made his name as a leading British scholar of Arabic and Islam, Edinburgh may fairly claim to have been in the place where he first experimented the method of combining linguistic, historical and theological perspectives. It was from Professor Tritton that the young Montgomery Watt was to have his first instruction in Arabic in the early 1940s. The Edinburgh lectureship in Arabic, independent of Hebrew, was created in 1912. Its first incumbent, Edward Robertson, was a bibliographer who published an authoritative guide to the collection of Arabic and Persian manuscripts held in the University Library.

But the real momentum in Arabic and Islamic studies in Edinburgh began with Robertson's successor, Richard Bell, who was appointed to the lectureship in 1921. Richard Bell has already been mentioned in connection with 'the Carlyle tradition' that inspired his vision of how to relate to Islam, a vision that he communicated to his student, William Montgomery Watt. Like Carlyle, Bell was attracted to the intellectual culture of Germany. In his case, however, it was less the romanticism of German poetry but the more rigorous disciplines of textual criticism, applied firstly to the Bible and then to the Qur'an, that attracted his interests.

German scholarship of Islam was at this time dominated by Theodor Nöldeke whose critical investigations into the dating and composition of the Qur'an were first published in 1860 under the title *Geschichte des Qorans*. Nöldeke's work marked the beginning of critical analysis of the Qur'an in the West, and was to shape the development of European Islamic scholarship for at least the next fifty years. Nöldeke's student, Friedrich Schwally, laboured to produce a second edition of his master's work, and eventually published it in two volumes in the early twentieth century. The second of these, dealing with the processes by which the verses and chapters of the Qur'an were organised into their present form, appeared in 1919 – just two years before Bell's appointment as lecturer in Edinburgh. It is scarcely surprising therefore that Bell decided to devote his own research to this area of scholarship, and in doing so he established a bridge between Scotland and Germany that was to prove important in the future of Islamic scholarship in Edinburgh.

Bell was no mere imitator of German approaches to the study of Islam. Originally trained in Christian theology, and an ordained minister of the Church of Scotland, he had a keen interest in the theological relationship between Islam and Christianity, especially in terms of the historical context of Qur'anic scripture and Muhammad's preaching. This was the subject of an important set of public lectures – the Gunning Lectures – that he gave in the Faculty of Divinity in 1925. Published in 1926 under the title of *The Origin of Islam in Its Christian Environment*, these explored the nature and development of Muhammad's understanding of Christianity. In contrast to most earlier forays into this topic that were driven by a priori assumptions of Muhammad's dependence upon the earlier religion – whether this was Judaism or Christianity depended largely on the protagonist's affiliation – Bell explored an entirely new approach based on his hypothesis that Muhammad had very little possibility of first-hand experience of either Judaism or Christianity, at least in the early development of his preaching in Mecca. Adopting and refining Nöldeke's periodisation of Qur'anic passages, he demonstrated a gradual internal development of Muhammad's preaching, from simple ethical monotheism with a strong emphasis upon thanksgiving to God as the Creator of all that exists, to a more elaborate outworking of this basic monotheism through the stories of prophets and rituals that he learned, mainly at second- or third-hand, from the oral traditions of Jewish and Christian communities in Arabia. Observing that eschatological beliefs in divine judgement, the punishment of Hell and the reward of Heaven, became more dominant as Muhammad's preaching developed in Mecca, Bell concluded that this suggested greater influence of Christian ideas, particularly in the Syriac Christian tradition that was predominant in northern Arabia. Yet he did not ascribe this to haphazard borrowing. Rather, it pointed to Muhammad's sophisticated interaction with Christian ideas, believing these to originate from the same divine source as his own preaching. It was only later, once Muhammad was established in Medina, that – according to Bell – he began to differentiate his religious teaching from that of both Christianity and Judaism, as he became more familiar with these, at first hand, in the later part of his career.

On the basis of these findings, Bell concluded that:

> We have, in fact, to allow for considerable originality in Muhammad, not the originality which produces something absolutely new, but the originality of a strong mind, working upon very imperfect information of outside things, yet finding expression for ideas and aspirations which were dimly present in their minds. He claimed to be an Arab prophet, and he was. We . . . see him consciously borrowing – he is quite frank about it.

But to begin with, the materials which he uses, though they may remind us ever and again of Jewish and Christian phrases and ideas, are in reality Arab materials.

Given that Bell's views about the nature and development of Muhammad's preaching depended on careful analysis of the internal evidence of the Qur'an itself, it is logical that he should have turned to a closer study of the Qur'an as his next project. It was to preoccupy the rest of his life. For the next two and a half decades he worked assiduously on an English translation of the Qur'an that was published in 1935, and on an interpretative introduction to the Qur'an's textual history and content, published in 1953, the year after his death. Singly the most important feature of this research was Bell's original approach to the chronological ordering of Qur'anic verses. He now went much further than Nöldeke, seeking to be much more precise as to the dating of verses within the different periods of composition that Nöldeke had outlined. He hypothesised that Muhammad may well have revised and added to the verses of one period as his career developed through later periods. This hypothesis was based on another: namely that, whilst Muhammad probably did not have the skill of writing – as Islamic orthodoxy claims – he made extensive use of secretaries who committed his 'revelations' to writing on scraps of 'paper', that is, any kind of writing material. If this is well enough established in the earliest biographical records of Muhammad's life, the novelty of Bell's hypothesis was the idea that unrelated passages of revelation were written down on different sides of a single piece of paper. This could explain why many sections of the Qur'an appeal suddenly to jump from one subject to another, without an obvious or logical relationship between them. Testing this hypothesis in a meticulous examination of all the verses of the Qur'an, Bell devised a complex reconstruction of the composition and dating of the entire Qur'an, and incorporated his conclusions in his 1937 publication, *Qur'an – Translated, with a Critical Rearrangement of the Surahs*. Referring to this monumental work in his inaugural lecture, Professor Watt praised it as 'a careful, painstaking work which has not yet been fully digested by scholars, and which will continue to be studied for many years to come'.

Watt also remembered how Mrs Bell spoke with great feeling of 'those ten terrible years' when her husband was buried in his translation work. But the work did not end with the translation. Over the next fifteen years Bell continued to elaborate his ideas in the form of a comprehensive introduction to the Qur'an that was published posthumously in 1953. Nearly twenty years later Professor Watt paid the highest tribute to his predecessor by publishing a revised edition of *Bell's Introduction to the Qur'an* that preserved the substance of Bell's original work, updating it in certain details and adding extensive bibliography to include more recent research. Likening this task to Friedrich Schwally's editorial revision and enlargement of Nöldeke's *Geschichte des Qorans*, Professor Watt wrote in his introduction to the new volume:

> The sincerest tribute to . . . a scholar is to take his views seriously and criticise them frankly. It is my hope that the present revision will enable a new generation of scholars to appreciate the importance of Bell's painstaking analysis of the Qur'an.

Nor was Professor Watt alone in admiring Richard Bell's work. Another of his students, Edmund Bosworth – later to become Professor of Islamic Studies at the University of Manchester, and an editor of the prestigious *Encyclopaedia of Islam* – was entrusted with an extensive typewritten manuscript in which Bell gathered the textual, grammatical and exegetical notes that accompanied his translation. His original intention had been to publish these in a compendium volume, but he died before this was possible.

The manuscript remained with the Edinburgh University Press for many years until Professor Bosworth was able to edit it for publication in two volumes, entitled *Commentary on the Qu'ran: Prepared by Richard Bell*.

This extended description of Richard Bell's work – considerably longer than the summary given in Professor Watt's lecture – is necessary to explain Professor Watt's remark that 'he (Bell) was one of the giants' of Islamic studies in the first half of the twentieth century, although 'a modest unassuming man' whose achievements were recognised by few of his Edinburgh colleagues in his own day. In addition to his writings, his influence should be recognised in the students whom he nurtured in this field, several of whom went on to develop distinguished academic careers. As well as Professors Watt and Bosworth, there was a third, Professor Sir Hamilton Gibb, who became, in Professor Watt's words, 'the doyen of Islamic studies in the English-speaking world'.

Born of Scottish parents in Egypt in 1895, the young Hamilton Alexander Rosskeen Gibb returned to Edinburgh for education in the Royal Grammar School from where he moved on to the university where he began his study of Arabic. This was in the earliest years of Richard Bell's teaching career, and their relationship was interrupted by the outbreak of World War I during which Hamilton Gibb served with the British forces in Europe. With the war over, he resumed his Arabic studies in London, where he quickly became a lecturer and later professor and editor of the *Encyclopaedia of Islam*. In 1937 he was appointed to the Laudian Chair of Arabic in Oxford, and eighteen years later to the professorship of Arabic in Harvard where he also directed the Centre for Middle Eastern Studies. During these years he published widely on social and religious aspects of Islam, and on Islamic literature; his book, originally entitled *Mohammedanism: an Historical Survey* (1949) and later re-titled as *Islam: an Historical Survey* (1980), served as the standard introduction to the subject through the middle decades of the twentieth century.

Islamic studies in the global arena

It is with a reference to Sir Hamilton Gibb that Professor Watt concluded his review of Scottish contributions to the development of Islamic studies in the West. The remainder of the lecture turns from 'retrospect' to 'prospect'. The striking, and perhaps regrettable, lacuna in this transition is any word about himself. While this may reflect the quality of modesty that he admired in his predecessor, it deprives his analysis of Islamic studies in Edinburgh of the enormous contribution that he made between his appointment to the lectureship in 1947 and his elevation to the chair in 1964. Of this period he merely states that Arabic and Middle Eastern studies in Edinburgh benefited from two British government commissions, the Scarborough Commission of 1947 and the Hayter Commission of 1961, that designated the University of Edinburgh as a centre for the development of Middle Eastern and African studies respectively. The single lectureship in Arabic was quickly developed into a department of Arabic and Islamic studies that included lectureships in Persian, Turkish, and, for a time, Urdu. While the Hayter Commission was primarily concerned with African studies, it was seen in Edinburgh as an opportunity to develop the study of African Islam. Commenting on this in his inaugural lecture, Professor Watt noted the significance of Islamic history in Africa from the Middle Ages, and its expanding influence in modern times. He predicted:

> By the end of the century it is likely that Islam will be the dominant religion of Africa: and, partly because of this, it is in Africa that the most interesting developments within Islam are to be expected during the next few decades.

This prediction did not reckon sufficiently with the enormous growth of African Christianity during the twentieth century, as a result of which Islam and Christianity figure as the two equally dominant religions in Africa today. But this serves only to make Professor Watt's point more firmly: that many of the most significant developments in religion are taking place beyond their traditional regions of dominance. Historically, Arnold Toynbee's analysis of world cultures held good. He identified five major cultural zones – Western civilisation with its roots in Western Christianity, the Orthodox Christian zone of south-eastern Europe and Russia, the Hindu zone of South Asia, the Far East with its dominant Buddhist and Confucian traditions, and the Islamic cultural zone stretching from West Africa through the Middle East to Malaysia and Indonesia. These were by-and-large self-contained cultural regions, although the nineteenth and early twentieth centuries saw the global expansion of Western or Euro-American civilisation. But with the collapse of European imperialism following World War II a new global reality emerged. Notwithstanding the global dominance of science and technology, the many different cultures of the world are reaffirming their identities, not only in their traditional zones of influence, but through complex processes of interaction with other cultures, resulting in a greater mix of people from different cultural backgrounds than at any previous time in world history. Professor Watt argued that: 'Just as all states are on an equal footing in the United Nations, so there is an equality in the cultural field in the sense that we have to approach as equals those from other cultural backgrounds.'

It is with this challenge that Professor Watt drew his inaugural lecture to a close. The Scarborough and Hayter commissions were 'chiefly practical and utilitarian' in their motives and recommendations, recognising that British government, industry, and commerce needed greater information and access to greater expertise on Africa and Asia. He recognised also that British universities benefited from the influx of international students. But, he argued, the university's response to this challenge is inadequate if it is confined only to such pragmatic considerations:

> A university must surely look beyond this and envisage some deeper study of non-European cultures. Such study, too, can no longer be left to a few enthusiasts or eccentrics, but must be widely spread among university graduates. It seems probable that by the year 2000 no man will be considered truly educated unless he has engaged at university level in some study of a non-European culture . . . Perhaps we should look forward to the time when the greatest works of Islamic and other Asian cultures are read and respected along with those of Greece and Rome as 'classics' of the 'one world'.

Professor Watt did not elaborate the methods by which the goal could be achieved, except in emphasising that there are no shortcuts. The process should begin as the normal part of school education, and the learning of the languages of Africa and Asia is essential both at school and university levels. So, he concluded his lecture with a direct appeal to the headmasters and headmistresses of Scottish schools to introduce the teaching of Arabic – or Chinese or Sanskrit – into the educational curricula. If these recommendations are less startling today, given the development of greater multicultural awareness in the late twentieth century, than they were in the mid-1960s, it remains undeniably true that the study of non-European cultures continues to struggle for a more central place in the attentions of most European universities.

Not only was Professor Watt among the pioneers in recognising and addressing of the challenges of the world in which cultures are interdependent; his vision remains a vital challenge today. In this sense, he deserves to be considered among the forerunners of contemporary post-colonialism, at least in his desire to move away from the Eurocentric view of the world, toward a creative interaction among cultures from which Westerners have as much to learn and to all other peoples. His path to the goal lay in the development of Islamic studies, with 'the hope' – to quote the concluding words of his lecture – 'with the hope that Scotland may play a worthy part in the continuing work of bringing Europeans and Americans to a deeper appreciation of the values of Islamic culture'.

Conclusion: 'the Carlyle Tradition'

If Professor Watt's inaugural lecture offered an overview of the 'worthy part' that Scottish scholars played in this task, the elaborations provided in this chapter have attempted to clarify the character of the intellectual legacy to which Professor Watt stood heir. It can be said, in conclusion, that several characteristics stand out quite clearly. For the most part, Scottish scholars showed a high degree of respect for Islam and Islamic civilisation, recognising their valuable contributions to both global and European culture. Their interests went beyond mere description, and sought to engage their subject in ways that could be mutually beneficial to Muslims and Westerners alike. If Thomas Carlyle symbolised this approach in a brilliant flourish of rhetoric, the so-called 'Carlyle tradition' goes back much further than Carlyle himself, to the first Scottish scholar of Islam, Alexander Ross. In this sense, it was 'original' to the Scottish way of engaging Islam, and sharply contrasts the Scottish approach to centuries of medieval negativity toward Islam that flourished elsewhere in Europe, including England.

As Carlyle's vision may be said to have inspired later Scottish scholars, their scholarship went much further than Carlyle in establishing this tradition on firm intellectual foundations. This involved primarily the study of Islamic texts, firstly those pertaining to the origins of Islam in the Qur'an and the life of the Prophet

Muhammad, and subsequently classic texts of Muslim civilisation. Scottish scholars led the English-speaking world in applying higher criticism to these ancient texts, not with the intention of disqualifying their value, but rather to understand them freshly through the methods of modern scholarship. This included what is today termed the 'contextual' study of texts, examining them in their social context, to draw out the complex interaction between intellectual and social factors in the evolution of meaning. It is also evident that many of the Scottish scholars of Islam were specifically interested in the relationship between Islam and Christianity as religions. While the missionary scholars displayed a theological bias in favour of Christianity, others – preeminently Richard Bell – postponed theological judgement while pursuing a thorough historical and textual exploration of the Christian–Muslim relationship.

This, then, is the Scottish tradition of Islamic scholarship into which Professor Watt had been inducted by his teacher, Richard Bell, and of which he became the principal exponent from the time of his appointment as University Lecturer in Arabic and Islamic Studies in 1947.

Note

1. Professor David Kerr worked tirelessly to promote greater understanding between Christians and Muslims. He greatly admired Professor Watt and that admiration was mutual. He was the Director of the Centre for the Study of Christianity in the Non-Western World at the University of Edinburgh from 1995 to 2005. He then moved to Lund in Sweden, where he was appointed to a chair in Missiology and Ecumenics. He died in 2008 at the age of 62.

APPENDICES

Appendix A: Some Reminiscences of Louis Massignon[1] (William Montgomery Watt)

I feel that the best tribute I can pay to the memory of Louis Massignon is to set down some of my personal memories of this great man. I first met him in Cambridge in 1954 at the International Congress of Orientalists. I was then a very junior Islamologist. We spoke about various things but not, so far as I remember, about my book *Muhammad at Mecca*, which had come out the previous year. What specially stands out in my memory is that, when he learnt I was from Scotland, he told me he was hoping to make a kind of pilgrimage to the birthplace of his friend Duncan Black Macdonald, which was in or near the island of Mull off [the] west coast of Scotland. I was able to give him details of trains, ferries and buses, and I put him in touch with Eric Bishop, then Lecturer in Arabic in Glasgow, who helped him with the 'transfer' across that city. I believe that he did in fact reach his goal and was well satisfied with having achieved this. I thought it was very typical of the man that he should be so interested in the particular geographical localities associated with some of the deep experiences of particular human beings. This is in line with the importance for him of the chapel in Brittany dedicated to the Seven Sleepers, and indeed with the importance of Mecca for Muslims and of the 'holy places' in Jerusalem for Jews, Christians and Muslims. I notice that Jacques Waardenburg in *Le Miroir*[2] says that Macdonald was born in Glasgow. If this is correct and Macdonald was not born in Mull, then the place Massignon wanted to visit must have had a formative influence on him in some other respect.

At Cambridge Louis Massignon invited me to call on him in Paris, and I did so several times in the following years. I gather that my visits did not differ greatly in character from those of other scholarly acquaintances. I would ring him up and he would give me a time, usually ten or eleven o'clock in the morning. There seemed to be an understanding that the visit would last for an hour. We would begin with an exchange of news and views, but before long he would launch into whatever subject was uppermost in his mind at the time, and there was nothing for me to do but listen. After the first visit I realised that, if I wanted to say to him something of importance, I had to get it out in the first ten minutes. On one or two of my visits he was going through a period of inner suffering because of the fighting in Algeria prior to the attainment of independence. Perhaps it was with reference to this that he once spoke of the efficacy of fasting.

In 1965 (or 1967) in Khartoum I met a Sudanese academic who had known him, and who described him as the one person he had met who was 'both a Muslim and a Christian'. This is a measure both of his positive appreciation of Islam and also of the depths of the friendships he was able to form with Muslims. Nowadays most Islamologists have Muslim friends, but Louis Massignon was one of the first of whom this was true. Nearly all his predecessors had been observers of Islam from without, most of them knowing it only from books. It is well known that Muslim friends played an important part in his return to the Christian faith he had lost. It would appear, too, that in the Qur'an and the writings of Muslim mystics he found fruitful material for his own meditations. The attraction of al-Hallaj[3] for him is obvious to all, but my personal feeling is that at some points he read more Christian truth into the life of al-Hallaj than is objectively justified. All in all, however, he made an immense contribution to a possible future reconciliation of Christianity and Islam.

At one point I told him of my deep interest in the life of Charles de Foucauld,[4] and on my next visit to him in rue Monsieur he showed me a letter Charles de Foucauld had written to him an hour or two before his death at Tamanrasset. I count it one of my great privileges to have been to Tamanrasset, to have seen the hermitage there and to have visited the cell in the nearby mountains. The visit to the cell was indeed almost a pilgrimage, and one in which most of the participants were Muslims. Mention of this letter reminds me that I have also seen some of Louis Massignon's correspondence with Constance Padwick,[5] and this contained among other matters descriptions of the crisis he went through before his return to Christianity.

As I come towards the end of my own life I become more concerned with the reconciliation of Islam and Christianity, and I believe in the probability of this happening. By reconciliation I mean not some syncretistic amalgam of doctrines, but a mutual recognition of their common goals by those seeking to serve God more fully; and I regard Louis Massignon's contribution to this reconciliation as one of the greatest.

Appendix B: A Tribute to Professor Watt[6] Professor (Josef van Ess, University of Tübingen)

When William Montgomery Watt wrote his PhD thesis on 'Free Will and Predestination in Early Islam', presented to the University of Edinburgh in 1944 and published four years later, in 1948, Islamic studies were still an undisputed *waqf*, 'endowment', of the Europeans. Certainly, there were some internationally renowned Islamists in the Arab world, in Turkey, in Iran and in the United States, but for the great scholarly tradition one was accustomed to look upon the English, the French, the Germans – to name only a few – who were then once again meeting on the battleground and applying their skill in the most 'relevant' way their governments could think of: by deciphering codes and performing secret missions behind the lines. In our days, more than thirty years later, Europe has become part of a larger world in this respect as well. Islamic studies, having established new outposts as far as Mexico and Australia, are drawing their energy from a constant dialogue with the Near Eastern countries; Muslims and Christians are mixing with one another as never before. The self-understanding of the 'Orientalist' could not remain unaffected. Only the governments seem to continue looking at him as somebody who might best be used in deciphering codes.

The methodical tool of European Orientalism was the 'hermeneutic circle', applied in what was normally called philology. This is how W. M. Watt started: his thesis demonstrated an unusual gift for textual interpretation, combined with a certain lucidity of arrangement which made the argumentation immediately clear to the reader. Yet there was more than sound method and persuasive style. There was also a feeling for the individuality of historical situations and ideological decisions which was not so common among philologists. Theology was not treated as an impersonal fight of ideas or, even worse, as a catalogue of notions and values, but as an expression of the way specific persons or groups reacted to the demands of their time. Traditional units ('the' Mu'tazila, 'the' Sunnis) were broken up into individual thinkers, the classifications of a biased heresiography reduced to their original meaning. This was far from pointillism or fragmentisation; the epochal forces and currents were always kept in mind. Islamic religion itself was put into its environmental context – for the first time, somebody pointed to the fact that certain predestinarian ideas formulated in *hadith* were nothing but residues of pre-Islamic fatalism, more or less adapted to the spirit of the new kerygma.

Two qualities had announced themselves: the ability to read a text as what it is, namely an *interpretation* of reality, not reality itself, and the abstraction necessary for defining the cipher of a movement or a period. Both qualities were brought to perfection during more than three decades of admirably productive scholarship. Their weight in relation to each other, however, became altered as a result of the slowly changing function of the Orientalist in society. There was the philological yeoman's work: a translation of a Christian Arabic text, the K*itab* al-*b*urha*n* written by

Eutychius, the Coptic patriarch of Alexandria in the early tenth century. There were a number of articles on early Islamic theology, Sunni as well as Shi'i, which opened the eye of the reader for the conditionality of doctrinal statements and apparently objective historical accounts. Yet, besides these pieces of detailed research which continued the approach used in the PhD thesis, there were, to a steadily increasing degree, summaries and introductions written for a larger reading public. This was not the result of mere chance or persuasion, as may happen nowadays where publishers of all sort are looking for victims compliant enough to write something general. It was consciously planned; W. M. Watt started a series with this intention at his own university press – a series, by the way, which has in the meantime acquired a high reputation. For he wrote not only for the sake of writing or for eternity, for the angels Abu-l-'Ala' al-Ma'arri was dreaming of in his *Risalat al-Ghufran*, and not even only for his colleagues – of whom there were not so many in his field anyway – but equally for educated people outside his discipline who wanted, or needed, to be enlightened about the 'Majesty that was Islam' and the reality it is in the present world. Even where he wrote for the insider he preferred to deal with the central personalities and the crucial problems: Muhammad, al-Ghazali, the 'integration' of Islamic society.

The two books on the life and the epoch of the Prophet, *Muhammad at Mecca* (1953) and *Muhammad at Medina* (1956), later on summarised in one single volume (*Muhammad: Prophet and Statesman*, 1961) and translated, in one or the other version, into several languages (French 1958–9, Turkish 1964, Spanish 1967, Japanese 1971), combined both qualities in die most fruitful way. It is true that the constant interplay of text and interpretation which characterised *Free Will and Predestination in Early Islam*, had disappeared; the enormous quantity of source material involved no longer allowed such a procedure. Yet there is a lot of word-by-word analysis, and the entire work is based on a thorough examination of the relevant reports. This was, however, not the only reason why it has rightly become a classic in the field of Muhammad studies. The philological detail was held together by new categories which were not so much derived from historical criticism, as had been the case in the famous biography by Frants Buhl, but rather from sociology and economic history. Watt left the angle of the usual historian of religions and tried to interpret the beginnings of Islam as a function of the *entire* situation of the time, not only by the religious circumstances prevailing at this moment. We may understand this as a simple inversion of the insight that Islam itself was not a religion in the sense of modern Christianity, mainly concerned with the 'inner self', but an attempt to shape society in its entirety. But there was more than that. W. M. Watt brought in such 'earthly' factors as economy: he asked himself the question, to what extent the change of religious consciousness which manifested itself in Muhammad's preaching reflected a change in the economic situation of Mecca. Even this question was not entirely new; no research about the Prophet of Islam could completely avoid it, and Hubert Grimme had dealt with it in a more detailed though somewhat premature and one-sided way long ago. But the formulation sounded Marxist, and this came as a shock to certain readers. Today the approach is current even in the most inveterate 'capitalist' milieu; twenty-five years ago it evoked some indignant comments.

This line of thought was taken up in *Islam and the Integration of Society* (1961). The project was enormous: an explanation of how Islam succeeded in incorporating the divergent elements which shaped its civilisation and how its initial pluralism developed into the uniform and almost monolithic worldview which characterised it until the intervention of modern European ideas. Faced with such an enterprise, philology had to step back. Sometimes, for instance in the chapter on the 'Islamization of West Africa', Watt works entirely on the basis of secondary literature. The way he chose for doing justice to his task was perhaps the only way possible, that is, illustrating the evolution by a few representative examples. The problem consisted in selecting the right examples and applying the right categories in their interpretation. The categories were the same as in his studies on Muhammad, and, as a matter of fact, the introductory chapter on the beginnings of Islam is largely an extract as well as a deepening of what had been said there. But now, in the broader context where these categories dominate much more than before, their origin is thrown into clearer relief. There is, again, the 'Marxist' approach, circumstantially discussed and carefully shaded, obviously under the impact of earlier criticism. But the main tool is the nomenclature typical for the sociology of religion as represented by Joachim Wach (the Kharijites as a 'community of saints') and, through him, by Max Weber (Shi'ism as the place of the 'charismatic leader') or the sociology of knowledge as it had been conceived by Karl Mannheim (the Assassins as a case of Islamic utopianism). These concepts were new for Islamic studies, more perhaps than in other fields. But sociology was expanding at supersonic speed in those days, and the booms caused by methodical and terminological exuberance tended to drown everything which went back to categories developed in the time between the two wars (and, moreover, not in Anglo-Saxon environments). The book remained a call in the wilderness; there was not much discussion and almost no attempt to carry it forward.

Islam and the Integration of Society had indicated a shift towards universality and, along with it, a certain impersonality. The traditional classifications elaborated by Muslim historiography which W. M. Watt had done so much to shake, were replaced by 'blocks' and 'currents' which seemed to fit the situation better. Yet the role of man in history was never neglected: Watt maintained the importance of the intellectual as an 'ideational' factor in society. He discussed the problem in a paradigmatic way in his small but profound study on al-Ghazali (*Muslim Intellectual*, 1963). He was not concerned with depersonalisation, as might have been suspected if he had followed another kind of sociology, but with coining handy formulas and concepts which could make Islam as a religion and Muslim civilisation as *a* whole understandable to an outsider. Seen under this aspect, the numerous surveys and introductions which followed – *Islamic Philosophy and Theology* (1962), *A History of Islamic Spain* (1965), *A Companion to the Qur'an* (1967), *Islamic Political Thought: the Basic Concepts* (1968), *What is Islam?* (1968), *The Influence of Islam on Medieval Europe* (1972), *The Majesty That Was Islam* (1974) – come as a logical consequence to what had announced itself before.

This reduction to the essential may be perceived in the double sense of the word: as a concentration or as a limitation and diminution; this is a matter of temper and standpoint. There is, of course, the danger of a certain repetitiveness and of a loss of contact with the sources – what scholar is not aware of this pitfall? W. M. Watt avoided it in his own way: by returning to the field he had treated in his PhD thesis, taking up what he had done in the meantime and putting it into a larger framework, thus forcing himself to add a vast amount of new material. The result was the best introduction into early Muslim theology we have up to now, his *Formative Period of Islamic Thought* (1973). The perceptivity for larger contexts had thus not pushed the detail aside, but integrated it into a more mature and more complex comprehension of reality. What this meant in fact had already become clear in the short study *Islamic Revelation in the Modern World* (1970). W. M. Watt had started to understand the historical evolution as a logical sequence of existential possibilities; he justified the alternatives of Islamic dogma as interpretations of commonly human – and therefore still relevant – religious phenomena by means of the 'categorial presuppositions' inherent in Islamic civilisation. By lifting these categorial presuppositions into the consciousness of the educated reader he fulfilled the obligation felt by every Islamist: to apply his *iftah ya simsim* to the treasures which he alone administers.

To W. M. Watt, this didactic or 'propagandist' mission was part of his vocation. He is a minister, and he has remained one through all his period of teaching. His first book, written in 1937, years before his PhD thesis, dealt with the question *Can Christians be Pacifists?* Simultaneously with his career as an Islamist, he published other works of this kind: *The Reality of God* (1957), *The Cure for Human Troubles* (1959), *Truth in the Religions* (1963). The colleague will normally know these books only, if at all, from the bibliography. But he should not neglect them: they offer some insight into W. M. Watt's methodical axioms (compare with, for example, his reflections on the sociology of knowledge in *Truth in the Religions*, pp. 6 ff.) and, above all, they explain the impetus of his personality. They explain his interest in Islam as a living reality; they explain, together with the influence of his teacher Richard Bell, his continuous preoccupation with the Qur'an (which does not go without saying among Islamists!), and they may explain why he, as a minister, was better acquainted with Marxism, the new religion of our age, than some of his colleagues. From the beginning, he saw his task as an Islamist in the dialogue; it was his destiny that he came to live in an ecumenical age. The dialogue was twofold: with his own society which, in happy ignorance, always tended to take its own values for granted, and with the Muslims who did just the same. This is why he tried to distil the fundamental notions of Muslim civilisation out of a recalcitrant mass of material; he wanted to make clear the alternatives which Islam, growing out of the same roots as Christianity, is able to offer. It is only with the awareness of these alternatives that a meaningful and unprejudiced dialogue can be started.

He performs this task with charity; whoever knows him knows how much his personality is shaped by this quality. Charity is perhaps indispensable to every philologist, as an antidote against the mercilessness of his business. But to W. M. Watt it means the ability to understand a culture on the level it deserves, by comparing its ideals with our ideals and its deficiencies with ours, without confusing both things in a hasty or, even worse, polemical way. In the dialogue he wanted, charity was equivalent to mediation, mediation between two partners who were not accustomed to talk to each other as friends. He found himself in the position of somebody who is, as he says in a revealing autobiographical remark, 'intellectually detached from both religions, while continuing to practise one'. In a kind of impartial sympathy, he tried to push forward the germs of community which are hidden in the axioms of both sides. Through his books, the Europeans – and Christians – have learnt that there are values and modes of life equivalent to theirs, similar in origin and intention, though dissimilar in their individual realisation, and the Muslims have felt understood without being unduly flattered. What else should an Islamist want for himself? It is his way of deciphering codes.

Appendix C: 'The Last Orientalist':[7] a Valedictory Interview with Professor Watt (Bashir Maan[8] and Alistair Mcintosh,[9] 1999)[10]

Professor Watt, how did you become interested in Islam and Christianity?
Well, I had studied Classics at Edinburgh University and 'Greats' – philosophy and ancient history – at Oxford. From 1934 to 1938 I taught moral philosophy at Edinburgh University. In 1937 when my mother died, I asked an Indian (later Pakistani) Muslim to come as a paying guest to help me pay for a housekeeper. Khwaja Abdul Mannan was a student of veterinary medicine and at that time, aged about twenty, a member of the Ahmadiyya Community – something he would have had to give up later when he became a colonel in the Pakistani army. Mannan, as he called himself, was an argumentative Muslim, and our many discussions over breakfast and evening meals raised my interest in the world of Islam. I believe that he is still alive in Lahore.

When I heard that the Anglican Bishop in Jerusalem wanted someone to work on Muslim–Christian relations I applied for the post. After studying theology and being ordained priest, I began to learn Arabic in London. Between 1941 and 1943 I completed my PhD at Edinburgh on freewill and predestination in early Islam. That was with Richard Bell, famous for translation of the Qur'an. Between 1944 and 1946 I worked in Palestine under the Bishop of Jerusalem. I had hoped to have discussions with Muslims, but Jerusalem proved not to be a good place to get in contact with intellectual Muslims. In 1946 things became difficult. I lost a friend when they blew up the King David Hotel. After leave I decided not to return to Jerusalem. In 1947 I became Head of the Department of Arabic and Islamic Studies at Edinburgh University and continued there until my retirement in 1979 at the age of seventy. In 1964 I received the title of Professor. I remain a priest in the Scottish Episcopalian Church and am presently writing another book about a Christian faith for today.

Your life's work has been devoted to dialogue between Islam and Christianity. Why is this important?
In the outburst of missionary activity around about the year 1800 the ideal was to go into the non-Christian parts of the world and convert everyone to Christianity; and this is still the ideal of some Christians. From Islam, however, there were very few converts. I have now come to doubt the appropriateness of conversion in many cases. The nineteenth-century missionaries did not appreciate the positive achievements of the great religions in giving their communities a tolerable and meaningful form of life. In the course of the years I have made many Muslim friends, some of them in influential positions. These persons are deeply rooted in their religion and are doing excellent work not only for their fellow-Muslims but also for wider circles. I would indeed admit that sometimes conversion may be necessary for an individual's spiritual health and growth; but this is exceptional. For such reasons I hold that the Christian aim for the foreseeable future should be to bring

the religions together in friendly dialogue and, where possible, in cooperation, for there is a sense in which all are threatened by the rising tide of secularism and materialism.

Many Westerners would question the value of dialogue with Islam because, for example, they see the Sharia as being cruel. Do you think this is true?
Well, similar punishments are found in the Old Testament – including, for example, the cutting off of women's hands in Deuteronomy 25. In Islamic teaching, such penalties may have been suitable for the age in which Muhammad lived. However, as societies have since progressed and become more peaceful and ordered, they are not suitable any longer.

If we demonise one another we cannot even debate such things. Dialogue is therefore imperative. It helps us to discern not just the meaning of the Holy Scriptures, but also the relevance that God wants them to have in our times.

What about the attitude of Muhammad (peace be upon him) towards women?
It is true that Islam is still, in many ways, a man's religion. But I think I've found evidence in some of the early sources that seems to show that Muhammad made things better for women. It appears that in some parts of Arabia, notably in Mecca, a matrilineal system was in the process of being replaced by a patrilineal one at the time of Muhammad. Growing prosperity caused by a shifting of trade routes was accompanied by a growth in individualism. Men were amassing considerable personal wealth and wanted to be sure that this would be inherited by their own actual sons. This led to a deterioration in the rights of women. At the time Islam began, the conditions of women were terrible – they had no right to own property, were supposed to be the property of the man, and if

the man died everything went to his sons. Muhammad improved things quite a lot. By instituting rights of property ownership, inheritance, education and divorce, he gave women certain basic safeguards. Set in such historical context the Prophet can be seen as a figure who testified on behalf of women's rights.

A lot also depends on what sort of Muslim society you look at. Many Westerners today think that Islam holds women in the heaviest oppression. That may be so in some cases, but only because they look at certain parts of the Islamic world. Pakistan, Bangladesh and Turkey have all had women heads of state. I therefore don't think the perception of Westerners is entirely correct.

What about war – Jihad versus Crusade? Terrorism, for example, can be considered both un-Islamic and unchristian, yet we see it justified by extremists whether in Egypt or Northern Ireland. Do you think violence can be part of faith?
Well, I think fundamentalists of any religion go beyond what their religion is about. But let me take an example from our Old Testament. I'm becoming very worried about the Old Testament because so much of it is unchristian. I read a passage every day and find it more and more so. There is a serious matter which is not clear from some translations. The *New Jerusalem Bible* that I read uses the phrase 'curse of destruction', and this was applied to towns when the Hebrews were coming into Palestine. They killed everyone in a town – men, women, children and sometimes also animals. This happened in Jericho as we see in Joshua 6, and in about a dozen other places; and there are also later instances. This is definitely unchristian.

I think on the whole Christianity is against war, though in the past Christians have supported wars. I don't think Islam is basically anti-Christian, but some extremists might take such a view.

There was a formal gathering of Scottish Christians and

Muslims at the national service of reconciliation in Edinburgh following the Gulf War a few years ago. Scottish church leaders had refused the government's wish to make it a service of 'thanksgiving'. They called it, instead, one of 'reconciliation'. The time of day coincided with the Muslims' evening call to prayer. At first the Muslims thought this would prevent them from attending. But then, to avoid any problem, they were allowed to say their prayers in St Giles Cathedral in front of the Christian altar while the Christian congregation kept silent. The following week Christians prayed in the community centre of the Glasgow Mosque. This would mirror the tradition that Muhammad allowed Christian delegations visiting him to pray in the mosque. Such a happening in modern Scotland, even after a war, suggests that religion can bridge the wounds of war.

I therefore certainly don't think the West is locked into Jihad with Islam, though I suppose if the fundamentalists go too far they'll have to be opposed. Iran's comments about the 'Great Satan' were aimed mostly at the United States: they were not made because the West was Christian. I think the West should try to overcome these strains between different religious groups. I do, however, think that the US is following a very dangerous policy in relation to the Middle East. The root of this trouble is that the US gives too much support to Israel. They allow them to have nuclear weapons and to do all sorts of things, some of which are contrary even to Jewish law. Jewish families occupy Arab houses without payment. That is stealing. I think that the US should be much firmer with Israel and put a lot of pressure on them, though this is difficult because of the strong Jewish lobby. Unless something is done there'll be dangerous conflict in the Middle East. Such danger would be less likely to arise if all three Abrahamic faiths – Jews, Christians and Muslims – paid greater respect to what God teaches us about living together.

Do you think that the newly re-established Scottish Parliament should take any position on the Middle East?
The Scots Parliament should keep to a middle course and certainly not join the anti-Islamic side. I'm sure it would like to see some balance of Jews and Muslims in the Middle East, and of course, fair treatment for the Palestinian Arabs, some of whom are Christian. The Scottish Parliament might try and help them to come to terms with one another.

Within Scotland, the parliament should work for some harmony between religions as there are Muslims and Jews, as well as Christians, in Scotland. With luck there'll be one or two Muslim MSPs. The big question is whether the Nationalists will win and go on to demand independence which I think might be a good thing, though I'm neither strongly for or against independence.

Islam maintains that the word of God is final and we can't change it. Christianity, with its understanding of the dynamic presence of the Holy Spirit, is in constant flux. Where do you stand on this difference?
I would be inclined to say that the Qur'an is the word of God for a particular time and place and will not therefore necessarily suit other times and places. The prohibition on usury may have been good for a certain time and place but that doesn't mean it will always be good.

You see, I think that Muslims need help in reaching a fresh understanding of the Qur'an as God's word, but comparison with the Bible does not help much. The Qur'an came to Muhammad in a period of less than twenty-five years, whereas from Moses to Paul is about 1,300 years. Christians could perhaps show from the Bible that there is a development in God's relation to the human race. For example, Moses was told to order the death penalty by stoning for anyone who broke the Sabbath by gathering firewood on it.

Joshua was told to exterminate the whole population of various towns – men, women and children. Could the loving God taught by Jesus have given such barbaric and bloodthirsty orders? To say 'No', as one would like to do, throws doubt on the inspiration of the Bible. We seem to have to say that the precise commands which God gives to believers depend on the form of society in which they are living. Traditionally Muslims have argued from God's eternity that the commands he gives are unalterable, and they have not admitted that social forms can change.

I therefore do not believe that either the Bible or the Qur'an is infallibly true in the sense that all their commands are valid for all time. The commands given in both books were true and valid for the societies to which the revelations were primarily addressed; but when the form of society changes in important respects some commands cease to be appropriate, though many others continue to be valid. I do, however, believe that Muhammad, like the earlier prophets, had genuine religious experiences. I believe that he really did receive something directly from God. As such, I believe that the Qur'an came from God, that it is divinely inspired. Muhammad could not have caused the great upsurge in religion that he did without God's blessing. The diagnosis of the Meccan situation by the Qur'an is that the troubles of the time were primarily religious, despite their economic, social and moral undercurrents, and as such capable of being remedied only by means that are primarily religious. In view of Muhammad's effectiveness in addressing this, he would be a bold man who would question the wisdom of the Qur'an.

What do you think of the Qur'anic statement that the Old Testament has been changed, thus accounting for some of the differences between the Abrahamic faiths?
Well, I think that the later writers sometimes changed earlier things to make them more suitable for their contemporaries. I think there

was a lot of rewriting of the Old Testament, though the form in which we have it hasn't been changed since the Christian era. I see the Old Testament as the record of a developing religion. As a religion develops some of the earlier stages may have to be abandoned completely. An example might be Islamic teachings on usury. I don't see how it is possible completely to get rid of usury. We'll have to see how Islamic attempts to get rid of usury work. Undoubtedly capitalism has got to be restricted in various ways. The world is certainly in a mess at the moment, but how we can get out of it, I don't know. All I can say is that there are things that Christianity can learn from Islam, especially on its spiritual side, and Islam can perhaps learn from Christian understanding of God in relation to the universe and human life. I think Muslims would find that this might give a slightly greater emphasis to something in their own faith.

I think another thing is that we have all got to come to terms with the scientific outlook of today. That is very critical of the Old Testament. The Old Testament says a lot about God's anger which I think is based on some of the false ideas that the Old Testament people had. They thought, you see, that God could interfere with the laws of nature. They thought that God made the sun stand still for a whole day so that Joshua could get a great victory. Well, that's impossible. They thought that God could intervene with His own natural laws and punish people. Well, I think there is a sense in which wrongdoing is punished, but even in the Bible it is recognised that the wicked sometimes flourish. There are different strands of thinking in the Bible.

Islam requires belief in God as revealed in 'the books' – not just the one book. This arguably incorporates Christian and Jewish scriptures. What, then, do you think Judeo-Christian understandings might have to teach Islam?

I think Muslims will have to take the work of Christ more seriously, even if they simply regard him as a prophet. The view I take, in accordance with the creeds, is that he was truly human. He wasn't a superman. That leaves you with the question of how he was also divine, but I think we have to look much more at his humanity. I also don't think he was able to work miracles except for those that other saints could also do – such as curing the sick. I don't think some of the other miracles really happened. For instance, one of the outstanding things was the supposed changing of water into wine at a marriage feast. This is given in the fourth Gospel and is said to be the first of the signs of Jesus' achievement. Clearly, this was meant to be understood symbolically, because making a lot of wine has nothing to do with the Gospel. It was meant to symbolise changing something ordinary into something precious, which is what Jesus had achieved. It was not meant to be taken literally – there was a tremendous amount of wine involved – the equivalent of about 900 bottles – and I don't think Jesus was an alcoholic.

In the Qur'an there is very little knowledge of Judaism and almost none of Christianity, except about such points as the virgin birth. There are references to Moses and Abraham and so forth, but nothing about, for example, the settlement of Israel in Palestine and the achievements of the later prophets with their important emphasis on justice. I cannot believe that God would not bless the development of greater awareness among Muslims of these things.

And what can Islam teach Christianity?

Speaking personally, it has taught me to think more deeply about the oneness of God. I am not happy with the traditional Trinitarian

Christian formulation of God comprising three 'persons' – Father, Son and Holy Spirit. The word 'person' has changed since it was first used in English four centuries ago. It was a translation of the Latin 'persona' – a face or mask, such as that used by actors. Now the English word means an individual, which is different. Christianity is not trying to say that God comprises three individuals. Islam, with its many different names for the qualities of God, can help the Christian see a more true meaning of Trinitarian doctrine. The Trinity is different faces or roles of the same one God. For me, that insight has been a direct result of my study of Islam.

There is a prayer that you have long used that brings together the Judeo-Christian with the Islamic before the God of us all. Might we close our interview with that?

O Father, Son and Holy Spirit, one God, grant that the whole house of Islam, and we Christians with them, may come to know you more clearly, serve you more nearly, and love you more dearly. Amen.

Professor Watt, thank you, so very much.

Appendix D: A Tribute to Professor Watt (Hakim Mohammed Said)[11]

Eminent are his works and respectably original views, though many readers may not wholly agree with all his interpretations at places. Religion, let us grant, is a subject in which different people even of the same school of thought may think differently according to their lights. But here in Professor Montgomery Watt's works, a balance is the built-in quality.

Reasonably assiduous effort to further the understanding of another people's religion demands a generous heart and an open mind, and in this respect Professor Montgomery Watt has demonstrated his scholarly magnanimity amply.

Yet the dedication of this volume to him is not enough tribute. As a scholar and a friend, I have always admired the qualities of his head and heart. I hold him in very high esteem.

Appendix E: William Montgomery Watt and a Historicist Interpretation of Islamic History (Hasan Hüseyin Adalioğlu)[12]

The views put forward by Western Orientalists with regard to some aspects of early Islamic history have been taken seriously in the Islamic world and gave rise to numerous rejections by the Islamists. What made William Montgomery Watt different from the preceding Orientalists is that he introduced relatively different approaches to the religious identity of the Prophet and the current theories and arguments about the economic, social and political organisation of Islam. The major characteristic of the theory developed by William Montgomery Watt is that he maintained his belief in Christianity and adopted a historicist approach to Islamic history while he at the same time accepted the religious identity of the Prophet Muhammad (peace be upon him) and declared that he had seen the message of the Prophet as a mere revelation from God. Indeed, he has not considered the Prophet only as a figure reacting under the influence of religious and external cultural factors, just to the contrary, he saw him as a person reacting against a social environment. Thus, Watt tried to analyse the social structure of

Mecca of the time sociologically and psychologically and attempted to account for the political teachings of the Prophet, which were fit for the social structure of his environment, from the perspective of an historicist.

Appendix F: Obituaries of William Montgomery Watt

i. Professor Hugh Goddard, University of Edinburgh[13]

Among British writers on Islam in the twentieth century, Montgomery Watt was exceptional, partly because of the range of his interests and the prolific volume of his publications, but more particularly because of the originality with which he approached certain crucial aspects of Islam, particularly the life of the Prophet Muhammad. The fact that his three main volumes on this topic, *Muhammad at Mecca*, first published by Oxford University Press in 1953, *Muhammad at Medina* (1956), and then *Muhammad: Prophet and Statesman* (1961), essentially a one-volume abridgement of the other two, have been kept more or less continually in print by OUP, the first two by OUP Pakistan, is perhaps the most fitting testimony to both the originality and the accessibility of his works.

Watt was born in Fife in 1909 and, like Muhammad, grew up as an orphan, his father, a Presbyterian minister, having died not long after his birth. His schooling was at George Watson's College in Edinburgh, and he went on to study Classics at the University of Edinburgh and then Greats at Balliol College, Oxford, before returning to the University of Edinburgh to teach moral philosophy from 1934–8. It was round about this time that two encounters which were to influence the whole of his subsequent career took place: firstly, following his mother's death, he took in a lodger who was an Ahmadi Muslim, Khwaja Abdul Mannan, and their conversations over breakfast and dinner evidently stimulated his interest in the faith and world of Islam; and secondly, he heard that the Anglican Bishop in Jerusalem, Graham Brown, was looking for someone to work as his academic adviser on Muslim–Christian relations. Watt, who had been ordained in the Episcopal Church of Scotland in 1939, applied and was accepted. He studied Arabic in London, while serving as a curate in St Mary's, The Boltons, and then returned to Edinburgh to study under Richard Bell, the translator and commentator on the Qur'an, for his PhD, which was completed in 1943 on the theme of 'Free Will and Predestination in Early Islam'.

Watt worked in the Middle East for three years, but by 1946 life was getting pretty difficult in what was then Palestine, and when a friend of his was killed in the blowing up of the King David Hotel in Jerusalem in that year he decided not to return after leave. Instead he returned to the University of Edinburgh, where he lectured in ancient philosophy for a year and then became Lecturer in Arabic in 1947. The rest of his career, apart from periods as a visiting professor in Canada, France and the United States, was then spent in the same department in the same institution, where he became Professor of Arabic and Islamic Studies in 1964, and it was there that, until his retirement in 1979, his formidable list of books and articles on different aspects of Islam was produced.

Edinburgh already had a distinguished tradition of Islamic

studies in general, and of the study of the life of Muhammad and of the Qur'an in particular, going back to Sir William Muir, who served as Principal of the University after a long career in the Indian Civil Service, and who wrote his own *Life of Muhammad* in four volumes between 1858 and 1861, and to Watt's teacher Richard Bell. During Watt's period as head of the department, however, its reputation was further enhanced, and the procession of PhD students from different parts of the Islamic world who came to study under his supervision is clear evidence of this. The fact that alongside all this activity and all the responsibilities involved with it he managed to be so productive in terms of publication is little short of remarkable, and he also found time to chair learned societies such as the Association of British Orientalists (1964–5). He continued to write prolifically after his retirement, and he was also generous in responding to requests for advice from other institutions in the UK which were thinking of developing the study of Islam, such as the University of Nottingham.

Selecting one or two of his publications for particular discussion is not an easy task, but alongside his work on Muhammad and the Qur'an his work on the development of Islamic theology and philosophy has been hugely influential: when his *The Formative Period of Islamic Thought* was first published by Edinburgh University Press in 1973 undergraduates studying the subject at the University of Oxford were told that they would not need to read anything else! His studies of the later Muslim theologian al-Ghazali have also been widely admired, and his translation of two works by al-Ghazali, his spiritual autobiography and a short work on the proper practice of Islam, under the title *The Faith and Practice of al-Ghazali*, first published in 1953, also remains in print.

Watt's publications were not limited to the historical study of Islam, however. He also wrote *Islamic Fundamentalism and Modernity* (1988), *Islam and Christianity Today: a Contribution* to Dialogue (1983), *Muslim–Christian Encounters: Perceptions and Misperceptions* (1991), a particularly valuable survey of the ways in which Christians and Muslims have interpreted, and often misunderstood, each other over the course of the centuries, and a number of works in which he expounded his liberal vision of the Christian faith, such as *Truth in the Religions: a Sociological and Psychological Approach* (1963) and *A Christian Faith for Today* (2002).

A volume of his collected articles published in 1990, *Early Islam*, is clear evidence of the wide range of his interests, including as it does valuable studies of such topics as the vexed question of whether or not the Qur'an states that Jesus prophesied the coming of Muhammad (based on 61:6 of the Qur'an), the early development of Muslim attitudes towards the Bible, and the question of whether or not, according to Islamic Theology, humanity is created in the image of God. Perhaps his most lasting legacy, however, will be the series which he established with Edinburgh University Press in 1962, the *Islamic Surveys*. He contributed several volumes to this series himself, on the Qur'an, on Islamic philosophy and theology, on the creeds of Islam, on Islamic political thought, on Islamic Spain, and on the influence of Islam on medieval Europe, and the series as a whole remains one of the most popular and accessible introductions to many different aspects of Islam for English-speaking readers.

His contribution to scholarship was recognised on both sides of the Atlantic, by the award of the eighth Giorgio Levi Della Vida Medal by the University of California in Los Angeles in 1981, and the award of the first British Society for Middle Eastern Studies prize for outstanding scholarship in 2002. Throughout his life Watt remained a priest of the Episcopal Church in Scotland, and from 1960 he was also a member of the ecumenical Iona Community. Muslim commentators have sometimes taken issue with some of his interpretations, as in Jabal Buaben's *Image of the*

Prophet Muhammad in the West: a Study of Muir, Margoliouth and Watt (1996). Few would deny, however, the extent to which he succeeded in moving Christian discussion on, particularly with reference to the person of Muhammad.

ii. Richard Holloway, Bishop of Edinburgh[14]

Professor William Montgomery Watt, who has died aged ninety-seven, was a legendary figure among Islamic scholars. He dedicated his life to the promotion of dialogue between Christians and Muslims. Of his many publications, he is most famous for three books on the Prophet Muhammad, acknowledged by experts to be classics in the field.

William was born in Ceres, Fife, where his father, who died when he was fourteen months old, was a minister. In an unpublished manuscript, William meditated on the impact of his father's death on his own attitude to life. It had necessitated a fair amount of moving about in his early years, and he mused: 'I sometimes wonder if this early change of abode is the source of my tendency, once I have found a tolerable billet, to remain in it as long as possible.'

If stability of life supplied emotional foundation, the other powerful drive was intellectual and spiritual exploration. He was educated at George Watson's College, Edinburgh, and at Edinburgh and Oxford Universities, where he took three degrees in six years: classics at Edinburgh, and Lit. Hum. and BLitt (for a thesis on Kant) at Oxford. He spent the 1934 summer semester studying philosophy at Jena, Germany.

William discovered Islam in 1937. While studying for a doctorate at Edinburgh, in order to make ends meet he took in a Muslim lodger, K. A. Mannan, a veterinary student from Pakistan and a member of the Ahmadiyya sect. 'I began to learn something about Islam, of which I had been largely ignorant,' William wrote later. 'But the dominant impression was that I was engaged not merely in arguing with this individual but in confronting a whole, century-old system of thought and life.'

This discovery led him to correspond with the Anglican Bishop in Jerusalem, George Francis Graham Brown. Brown became something of a father figure to William, who agreed to join him in Jerusalem as his chaplain, working on the intellectual approach to Islam. This meant that he had to seek ordination in the Anglican Church; he was fast-tracked through Cuddesdon Theological College in a year, and ordained deacon in 1939. He served a curacy at St Mary's, The Boltons, Kensington, and began studying Arabic at the School of Oriental Studies. He was ordained in 1940, and after St Mary's was closed because of bomb damage, returned to Edinburgh to finish his training as a curate at Old St Paul's, and begin work on his doctoral thesis, 'Free Will and Predestination in Early Islam'. He finally made it to Jerusalem in 1943.

After returning to Scotland in 1946, William became Lecturer in Arabic at the University of Edinburgh, where he remained until his retirement in 1979. He was given a Personal Chair in Arabic and Islamic Studies in 1964, and it was during this time that he produced *Muhammad at Mecca* (1953), *Muhammad at Medina* (1956) and *Muhammad: Prophet and Statesman* (1961), a popular abridgement of the previous two books.

William said of his commitment to the study of Islam that he always had an ability to see the other person's point of view – 'indeed, almost a tendency to prefer the other's point of view'. He became fascinated by the historical prejudice of the west against Islam, which Norman Daniel, author of *Islam and the West: the Making of an Image*, made clear to him had been created by twelfth–fourteenth-century scholars as war propaganda in support of the Crusades. William came to the conviction that the distorted image was a negative aspect of European identity, that is, an image of what the European is not. It is then in contrast to his positive identity as a Christian. The tenacity of the prejudice I would attribute to the fact that the distorted image was an essential aspect of the emergence of European identity.

While he remained a Christian, and worked for many years as a priest for the Scottish Episcopal Church, there was a time, under the influence of Charles de Foucauld, the French priest who lived among Algerian Muslim tribes until his assassination in 1916, when William thought of his vocation as constituting 'a willed and deliberate presence' in the intellectual world of Islam. To implement this conception of presence, he often took as the basis for his daily meditation a passage from the Qur'an or an Islamic mystical work. He brought the same exploratory reverence to his own Christian faith.

Despite his Anglicanism, William retained enormous respect for the Presbyterian tradition, and respected the decision of his wife, Jean, whom he married in 1943, to become a Catholic. He joined the Iona Community in 1960, because he found its brand of radical, exploratory faith congenial. Indeed, he continued to be both an explorer and a theological reconciler to the end. His last book, *A Christian Faith for Today*, published in 2002 when he was ninety-three, was a distillation of the sort of generous Christianity to which he had given his life.

iii. Professor Carole Hillenbrand[15]

W. Montgomery Watt, who in his long lifetime was probably the foremost non-Muslim interpreter of Islam in the West, was an enormously influential scholar in the field of Islamic studies and a much-revered name for many Muslims all over the world.

Born in Ceres, Fife, in 1909, William Montgomery Watt, like many other famous Scots, was a son of the manse. His father died while he was still a baby and he was brought up, as an only child, by his mother, uncle and aunt in Edinburgh. Educated at George Watson's College, he then studied at the universities of Edinburgh, Jena and Oxford.

Although he specialised initially in philosophy and theology, he became interested in Islam through lengthy conversations with an Indian lodger who was of the Ahmadi persuasion. His serious study of Arabic began with Richard Bell, the Edinburgh Orientalist. He was ordained in the Episcopalian Church in 1939. His subsequent appointment as chaplain to the Bishop of Jerusalem took his interest in Islam to a new level.

Soon after he returned to Scotland, he was appointed Lecturer in Arabic at Edinburgh in 1946; there he spent nearly all his long and fruitful career. He was awarded a personal chair in 1964 and he retired in 1979.

Unlike many famous Scots, Watt didn't seek his fortune south of the border, but settled in a charming house in Dalkeith, just outside Edinburgh, in 1947. There he and his wife, Jean (née Donaldson), whom he had married in 1943, enjoyed a long and happy life. As well as his academic duties, Watt continued as a serving minister of the Scottish Episcopal Church for many years until infirmity confined him to his home. He remained a member of the ecumenical Iona Community from 1960.

Watt's vast scholarly output – he wrote thirty-three books and scores of articles – has made his name renowned in the Middle East, the Indian subcontinent, Malaysia and Indonesia, as well as in the West. He was a towering figure in the history of Edinburgh University Press, establishing the highly successful *Islamic Surveys* series in 1962 to bring the subject to a wider readership, and writing seven books for that press, all of which are still in print and are among its bestsellers. His other books have been translated into a vast array of other languages.

His early books on Islam concentrate primarily on the career of the Prophet Muhammad. They are based on a close analysis of the original Arabic sources and the two works *Muhammad at Mecca* (1953) and, especially, *Muhammad at Medina* (1956) remain classic studies. *Freewill and Predestination in Early Islam* – the subject of his PhD – was published in 1948 and reveals an interest in Islamic theology which stayed with him all his life. He translated the spiritual 'autobiography' of the great medieval Muslim scholar Abu Hamid al-Ghazali (*The Faith and Practice of al-Ghazali*, 1953) and followed that with an excellent study of al-Ghazali entitled *Muslim Intellectual* (1963). Perhaps his finest achievement in the field of Islamic theology was his magisterial *The Formative Period of Islamic Thought* (1973). For these works on theology Watt relied not just on primary Arabic sources but, because of his excellent reading knowledge of German, he could draw on the great pioneering traditions of nineteenth-century German scholarship on Islam. Especially in his later years Watt's writing concentrated on an abiding concern of his – dialogue between Christians and Muslims – and in this field he published, for example, *Muslim–Christian Encounters: Perceptions and Misperceptions* (1991). He also published steadily on Christian topics and his own faith gave a spiritual dimension not just to his discussion of Christianity but also to what he said about Islam.

Watt was awarded many academic honours; he held visiting professorships at the University of Toronto, the Collège de France and Georgetown University, and received the American Giorgio Levi Della Vida Medal and was, as its first recipient, the British Society for Middle Eastern Studies award for outstanding scholarship.

Long before the recent wave of Islamophobia in the West, Watt advocated dialogue with Muslims, not demonisation of them. He doubted the appropriateness of conversion and felt that those of all faiths should collaborate in friendship to stem the tide of materialism and secularisation. Unlike certain Orientalist scholars of previous generations, Watt was indeed convinced that the Qur'an was divinely inspired and that Muhammad received true religious experiences directly from God. Watt roundly condemned those in the West who sought to perpetuate scurrilous medieval misconceptions about the Prophet of Islam.

He was not afraid to express rather radical theological opinions – controversial ones in some Christian ecclesiastical circles. He often pondered on the question of what influence his study of Islam had exerted on him in his own Christian faith. As a direct result, he came to argue that the Islamic emphasis on the uncompromising oneness of God had caused him to reconsider the Christian doctrine of the Trinity, which is vigorously attacked in the Qur'an as undermining true monotheism. Influenced by Islam, with its ninety-nine names of God, each expressing special attributes of God, Watt returned to the Latin word 'persona' – which meant a 'face' or 'mask', and not 'individual', as it now means in English – and he formulated the view that a truer interpretation of the Trinity would not signify that God comprises three individuals. For him, the Trinity represents three different 'faces' of the one and the same God.

Always a shy man, he enjoyed the simple life with his family, either in Dalkeith or in his summer home in Crail on the Fife coast, walking, gardening, stamp-collecting, and latterly, in extreme old age, he derived great pleasure from doing several crosswords a day.

iv. Ms Charlotte Alfred, a student of Islam at the University of Edinburgh in 2006[16]

William Montgomery Watt – 14 March 1909 – 24 October 2006: leading Islamic scholar, whose remarkable legacy is encountered at the University of Edinburgh, and across the Muslim world.

Professor Watt became interested in Islam while lecturing in moral philosophy at the University of Edinburgh in the 1930s. His mother had just died, and in order to pay for the housekeeper he invited an Indian Muslim to live as a paying guest in his house. Over breakfast and evening meals, passionate discussions between the two ignited his interest in Islam and the Arab world. This interest was to lead him all over the Muslim world, including working for the Bishop of Jerusalem from 1944 to 1946. His outstanding Islamic scholarship is world renowned, and the University of Edinburgh was one of its major beneficiaries. Between 1947 and 1979 he worked in Islamic and Middle Eastern Studies, contributing to its development into one of the most highly regarded departments in its field. He has written over thirty books, and bestowed his exceptional personal collection of 1,400 titles on the University of Edinburgh Library, covering Qur'anic commentary, mysticism and Islamic law, the history of the Arab world, and Arabic literature.

Professor Watt first came to Edinburgh to study Classics, and continued his studies in philosophy and ancient history at Oxford. He returned to Edinburgh to lecture in moral philosophy from 1934 until 1938, when he decided to complete a PhD on freewill and predestination in early Islam under Richard Bell, the pre-eminent Qur'anic scholar and Reader of Arabic at the university. His interest led him to Palestine, where he worked for the Bishop of Jerusalem from 1944 to 1946 as an Arabic specialist, on the topic of Muslim–Christian relations. He was frustrated by the lack of opportunities for intellectual exchange with Muslims at that time in Jerusalem and, when he lost a friend in the bombing of the King David Hotel, he decided to return to Edinburgh. From Lecturer in Ancient Philosophy from 1946–7, he became Lecturer, Senior Lecturer and then Reader in Arabic from 1947 to 1964. In 1964 he was offered the personal chair of the department, at that time named the Muir Institute, and oversaw its development into a centre of excellence for the study of the Muslim world. The departments of Arabic, Turkish and Persian were amalgamated into the Department of Islamic and Middle Eastern Studies. His leadership and academic renown played no small part in the development of this centre of learning at the university. The department professes that 'Edinburgh's present international reputation in the field of Islamic Studies is inseparable from the name of William Montgomery Watt'. He retired in 1979, but continued to publish titles into the late 1990s.

Professor Watt was highly regarded throughout the academic world. He held visiting professorships at the University of Toronto, the Collège de France, Paris, and Georgetown University and was awarded an honorary doctorate by the University of Aberdeen. He was also ordained into the Scottish Episcopalian Church in 1939 and became a member of the ecumenical community of Iona in 1960. The community's focus on ecumenism, as well as peace and justice issues, accord with his view that

> the Christian aim for the foreseeable future should be to bring the religions together in friendly dialogue and, where possible, in cooperation, for there is a sense in which all are threatened by the rising tide of secularism and materialism.

His views on Islam and Christianity have at times been controversial. He rejects the infallibility of both the Bible and the Qur'an, but regards each as divinely inspired. He has argued that the Muslim and Judaeo-Christian traditions have much to teach each other, personally commenting that his study of Islam deepened his understanding of the oneness of God. He has written extensively on Islamic politics, history and the role of women in Islam, among other topics. His works include *Muhammad: Prophet and Statesman* (1961), *Muslim–Christian Encounters: Perceptions and Misperceptions* (1991) and *Muslim Intellectual:*

a Study of al-Ghazali (1963). Professor Carole Hillenbrand, the current Head of the Department of Islamic and Middle Eastern Studies, attests to his remarkable legacy: 'Professor Watt was probably the foremost Western scholar on Islam in the twentieth century and he always sought to build bridges between Christianity and Islam.'

He died, at the age of ninety-seven, at his home in Dalkeith, survived by his wife Jean, their children, grandchildren and great-grandchildren.

Notes

1. Louis Massignon (d. 1962) was a very eminent French scholar of Islam. I am extremely grateful to Professor Watt's daughter Ann, who very kindly sent me a copy of her father's unpublished file about Massignon. She mentioned to me that Professor Watt had written a contribution about his reminiscences of Massignon in the proceedings of a conference, held in Cairo between 11 and 13 October 1983 to celebrate Massignon's centenary. Ann also told me that she did not know whether her father had attended the conference in person or whether he had just contributed his article.
2. This is a reference to a well-known book written by the Dutch scholar, Jacques Waardenburg: *L'Islam dans le miroir de l'Occident: Comment quelques orientalistes occidentaux se sont penchés sur l'Islam et se sont formé une image de cette religion*, The Hague, 1963.
3. Al-Hallaj, the famous Sufi who was crucified in Baghdad in 922, was the subject of Massignon's most famous book, *Akhbar al-Hallaj: Recueil d'oraisons et d'exhortations du martyre mystique de l'Islam*, Paris, 1975.
4. Charles Eugène de Foucauld was a French Catholic priest, who lived in the Sahara amongst the Tuareg in Algeria. He was killed in 1916.
5. Ann Watt mentioned to me that Constance Padwick, a British missionary and writer, was her godmother.
6. 'Tribute to Professor Watt', in *Islam: Past Influence and Present*

Challenge, eds. Alford T. Welch and Pierre Cachia, Edinburgh, 1979, ix–xiii.

7. In their preface to the 1999 interview, Bashir Maan and Alastair McIntosh mention that this title had been given to Watt by the Muslim press.
8. Dr Bashir Maan was a Scottish Representative on the Executive of the Muslim Council of Great Britain, was for eight years Chair of the Glasgow Central Mosque Committee and, as an elected Glasgow city councillor, he chaired the Strathclyde Joint Police Board, which, at that time, was Britain's second-largest police force.
9. Alastair McIntosh's work on 'combating Islamophobia' is part of the Edinburgh-based Centre for Human Ecology's Action for Transformation work, supported by the Quaker Concerns programme of the Joseph Rowntree Charitable Trust. He is an Associate of the Iona Community and from 1986 to 1990 was its business adviser.
10. Professor Watt was ninety when he gave this interview.
11. The Hamdard Foundation in Pakistan published a felicitation volume dedicated to Professor Watt in 1993. The book contained fourteen essays on Islamic subjects written in honour of Professor Watt by thirteen Muslim scholars and one non-Muslim: *Essays on Islam. Felicitation Volume in Honour of Prof. W. Montgomery Watt*, ed. Hakim Mohammed Said, Karachi, 1993, v–vi. The author of this tribute, Professor Hakim Mohammed Said, is a well-known Muslim scholar from Pakistan.
12. *İslâmî İlimler Dergisi, Yıl 3, Sayı 2, Güz 2008*, 33–46. Dr Hasan Hüseyin Adalioğlu is a contemporary Muslim scholar from Turkey.
13. Published in *The Scotsman* on 30 November 2006.
14. Published in *The Guardian* on 14 November 2006.
15. Published in *The Independent* on 8 January 2007.
16. Published in *Edinburgh Middle East Report Online*, Winter 2006.

A Bibliography of the Books Published by William Montgomery Watt[1]

Can Christians be Pacifists? (London: Student Christian Movement Press, 1937).
Free Will and Predestination in Early Islam (London: Luzac, 1948).
Muhammad at Mecca (Oxford: Clarendon Press, 1953).
The Faith and Practice of al-Ghazali (London: Allen & Unwin, 1953).
Muhammad at Medina (Oxford: Clarendon Press, 1956).
The Reality of God (London: SPCK, 1957).
The Cure for Human Troubles: a Statement of the Christian Message in Modern Times (London: SPCK, 1959).
Islam and the Integration of Society (London: Routledge & Paul, 1961).
Muhammad: Prophet and Statesman (Oxford: Oxford University Press, 1961).
Eutychius of Alexandria. The Book of the Demonstration (Kitab al-burhan), II. AR. 23. *Corpus Scriptorum Christianorum Orientalium* (Leuven: Peeters, 1961).
Islamic Philosophy and Theology (Islamic Surveys 1) (Edinburgh: Edinburgh University Press, 1962).

Muslim Intellectual: a Study of al-Ghazali (Edinburgh: Edinburgh University Press, 1963).
Truth in the Religions: a Sociological and Psychological Approach (Edinburgh: Edinburgh University Press, 1963).
A History of Islamic Spain (co-authored with Pierre Cachia) (Edinburgh: Edinburgh University Press, 1965).
A Companion to the Qur'an (London: Allen & Unwin, 1967).
What Is Islam? (London: Longmans Green and Beirut: Librarie Du Liban, 1968).
Islamic Political Thought: the Basic Concepts (Islamic Surveys 6) (Edinburgh: Edinburgh University Press, 1968).
Islamic Revelation in the Modern World (Edinburgh: Edinburgh University Press, 1970).
Bell's Introduction to the Qur'an: Fully Revised and Enlarged (Islamic Surveys 8) (Edinburgh: Edinburgh University Press, 1970).
The Influence of Islam on Medieval Europe (Islamic Surveys 9) (Edinburgh: Edinburgh University Press, 1972).
The Formative Period of Islamic Thought (Edinburgh: Edinburgh University Press, 1973).
The Majesty That Was Islam: the Islamic World, 661–1100 (London: Sidgwick & Jackson, 1974).
Islam and Christianity Today: a Contribution to Dialogue (London: Routledge & Kegan Paul, 1983).
Muhammad's Mecca: History in the Qur'an (Edinburgh: Edinburgh University Press, 1988).
Islamic Fundamentalism and Modernity (London and New York: Routledge, 1988).
Early Islam: Collected Articles (Edinburgh: Edinburgh University Press, 1990).
Muslim–Christian Encounters: Perceptions and Misperceptions (London: Routledge, 1991).
Islamic Creeds: a Selection (Islamic Surveys Series) (Edinburgh: University of Edinburgh, 1994).
Religious Truth for Our Time (Oxford: Oneworld, 1995).

A Short History of Islam (Oxford: Oneworld, 1996).
The History of al-Tabari (Ta'rikh al-rusul wa-l-muluk): Muhammad at Medina. Translated by Michael V. Macdonald and annotated by W. Montgomery Watt, Vol. VII (Albany: State University of New York Press, 1987).
The History of al-Tabari (Ta'rikh al-rusul wa-l-muluk): Muhammad at Mecca. Translated by Michael V. Macdonald and annotated by W. Montgomery Watt, Vol. VI (Albany: State University of New York Press, 1988).
A Christian Faith for Today (London and New York: Routledge, 2002).

Note

1. A full list of Professor Watt's published works until 1979 can be found in *Islam: Past Influence and Present Challenge*, the *Festschrift* edited by Alford T. Welch and Pierre Cachia and published in 1979 in his honour by Edinburgh University Press.

Index

References to notes are indicated by n

'Abd al-Malik, 33
Abraham, 11
Abu Bakr, 26
African studies, 100–1, 128–30
Alfred, Charlotte, 168–71
Arab identity, 33–4
Arabic language, 7, 114–15
Arabic studies, 87–9, 95–101, 107–8, 116–22
Arabs and Others in Early Islam (Bashear), 34
archaeology, 29–30
Augustine, St, 16
Ayoub, Mahmoud, 13

Balliol College, Oxford, 4, 59, 70–1
Bashear, Suliman, 34
Bayle, Pierre, 89
Becker, Carl Heinrich, 44n14
Believers, 35, 36
Bell, Richard, 5, 6, 63, 65, 75
  and Carlyle, 111
  and Islamic studies, 122–8
  and the Qur'an, 98–100
Bergsträsser, Gotthelf, 39–40, 42
Bible, the, 23, 148, 149, 151–4
Book of Demonstration, The (Eutychius), 10
Bosworth, Edmund, 126–7
Bosworth, George, 62, 63, 74
Bousquet, Georges-Henri, 21
British Society for Middle Eastern Studies, 6, 162
Brown, Peter, 28
Buaben, Jabal, 162–3
Buddhism, 81
Burns, James Golder (uncle), 68–9
Burns, John Campbell (grandfather), 67–8
Burton, John, 37
Byzantine Empire, 26, 29, 31–2

Cambridge University, 95–6, 114–17
Can Christians be Pacifists? (Watt), 5, 72, 144

176

Carlyle, Thomas, 91–3, 99, 109–12, 112–13, 114, 131–2
Casanova, Paul, 35
Caspari, Carl Paul, 114–15
Chalcedonian Christianity, 32
Christian Faith for Today, A (Watt), 51, 162, 165
Christianity, 10, 11, 13, 85–6
and Africa, 129
and Carlyle, 110
and God, 81–3
and Hellenism, 79–80
and Islam, 14–15, 16–17, 36, 108, 147–8, 149–50, 154–5
and Muhammad, 24, 32–3, 123–5
and Muir, 113–14
and pluralism, 78–9
and Watt, 15–16, 50–1, 60–1, 165
see also Bible, the; Nestorian Christianity
Church of Scotland, 4, 5
Cockburn, Norman, 61, 62, 73
Collège de France, 6
Columba, St, 88
Commentary on the Qur'an: Prepared by Richard Bell (Bosworth), 127
Conrad, Lawrence I., 23
consumerism, 84
Cook, Michael, 25–7, 28, 32, 34–5
Copts, 79, 80
Crone, Patricia, 25–7, 28, 32, 34–5
Crusaders in the East, The (Stevenson), 98
Crusades, 50, 89
Cuddesdon College, Oxford, 5, 49, 62, 74
culture, 80–1, 101–3, 129
Cure for Human Troubles: a Statement of the Christian Message in Modern Times, The (Watt), 13, 144

Dalkeith, 7, 51, 65
Daniel, Norman, 50, 164
Déroche, François, 41–2

Development of Muslim Theology, Jurisprudence and Constitutional Theory (Macdonald), 121
Dome of the Rock, 33
Donaldson, Jean *see* Watt, Jean

Early Arabic Historical Tradition: a Source-critical Study, The (Conrad), 23
Early Islam (Watt), 162
Edinburgh *see* University of Edinburgh
Egypt, 30, 31–2, 39, 80
Elwell-Sutton, Laurence, 62
Encyclopedia of Islam, 121, 126, 127
Ess, Josef van, 11, 16
Eutychius, 10, 140

Fables of Bidpai (Keith-Falconer), 119
Faith and Practice of al-Ghazali, The (Watt), 11, 161, 167
Fife, 7, 51
First World War, 68–9
fitna (civil war), 31
Flügel, Gustav, 39
Formative Period of Islamic Thought, The (Watt), 11, 143, 161, 167
Foucauld, Charles de, 50, 137, 171n4
Free Will and Predestination in Early Islam (Watt), 10, 167
fundamentalism, 149, 150

Gairdner, William Temple, 94, 118, 119–21
Gardner, William R. W., 93–4
Georgetown University, 6
Germany, 22–4, 39–40, 122–3
Geschichte des Qorans (Nöldeke), 123, 126
al-Ghazali, Abu Hamid, 11–12, 16, 120, 143, 161, 167
Gibb, Elias John Wilkinson, 96–7, 114, 116–17
Gibb, Sir Hamilton, 62, 100, 127–8
Gibbon, Edward, 91
Giorgio Levi Della Vida Medal, 6, 162

God, 14–15, 81–3
Goddard, Hugh, 159–63
Goethe, Johann Wolfang von, 92, 110, 113
Goldziher, Ignác, 22, 25
Gospels, the, 23
Graham, John Keddie (uncle), 69
Graham Brown, George Francis, 49, 50, 61, 64, 73, 75–6
Grammaire Arabe (Sacy), 115
Grammar of the Arabic Language, A (Wright), 114–15
Grammatica Arabica (Caspari), 115
Greece, 79–80, 82–3
Grimme, Hubert, 20, 141
Grohmann, Adolf, 29
Gunning Lectures, 123

Hagarism: the Making of the Islamic World (Crone/Cook), 25–8, 32, 34–5
Al-Hallaj, 137, 171n3
Hamniurabi, 88
Hayter commission, 100, 102, 128, 129
Hebrew studies, 98
Hero and Prophet, The (Carlyle), 114
Hijaz, 26
Hillenbrand, Carole, 165–8
Hinduism, 81
History of Islamic Spain, A (Watt), 12
History of Ottoman Poetry, A (Gibb), 96–7, 116
Hitler, Adolf, 71–2
Hogg, John, 93–4, 118, 119
Holloway, Richard, 163–5

Ibn Ishaq, 23
Image of the Prophet Muhammad in the West: a Study of Muir, Margoliouth and Watt (Buaben), 162–3
India, 113
Inferno (Dante), 88
Influence of Islam on Medieval Europe, The (Watt), 12
Introduction to the Qur'an (Bell), 99

Iran, 30, 150
Iraq, 8, 31
Islam, 3, 5
and Africa, 128–9
and Christianity, 82, 83, 85, 147–8, 149–50, 154–5
and Edinburgh, 122–8
and Massignon, 135–7
and missionaries, 93–5
and origins, 10–11, 21–36
and Scotland, 88–91, 131–2
and Watt, 9–10, 49, 50, 64–5, 138–45, 146–7, 157–8, 163–5
see also Arabic studies; Muhammad, Prophet; Qur'an, the
Islam: an Historical Survey (Gibb), 127–8
Islam and Christianity Today: a Contribution to Dialogue (Watt), 161–2
Islam and the Integration of Society (Watt), 11, 141–3
Islam and the West: the Making of an Image (Daniel), 50, 164
Islamic Creeds (Watt), 12
Islamic Fundamentalism and Modernity (Watt), 13, 161
Islamic Philosophy and Theology (Watt), 12, 19
Islamic Political Thought: the Basic Concepts (Watt), 12, 19
Islamic Revelation in the Modern World (Watt), 143
Islamic Studies in Scotland: Retrospect and Prospect (lecture), 3, 87–103
Islamic Surveys series, 12–13, 19, 162, 166
Islamophobia, 14, 17, 167–8
Israel, 16, 30, 150; *see also* Jerusalem

Jacobites, 79, 80
Jeffrey, Arthur, 39, 40
Jerusalem, 5–6, 16, 26, 49, 50, 61, 64–5, 75–6
Jesus Christ, 33, 78, 85–6, 162
Jihad, 149, 150

Jordan, 30
Judaism, 11, 26, 34–5, 79, 123–5

Kaegi, Walter, 26
Kant, Emmanuel, 4, 92
Keith-Falconer, Ion, 94–5, 118–19
Kemp Smith, Norman, 59, 71
Kerr, David, 132n1
Kinship and Marriage in Early Arabia (Robertson Smith), 96, 116

Lammens, Henri, 22
language, 79, 103, 114–15
Larkhall, 56–7, 68, 69
Late Antiquity, 28, 42
Laud, Archbishop, 89
Lawrence, T. E., 62
Lay of the Last Minstrel, The (Scott), 88
Lebanon, 30
Lectures on Comparative Grammar of Semitic Languages (Wright), 115
Lectures on the Religion of the Semites (Robertson Smith), 116
Leibniz, Gottfried Wilhelm, 92
Levant, the, 30
Life of Mahomet, The (Muir), 112, 161
Life of Muhammad, The (Sprenger), 112
Livingstone, David, 93, 118
Lüling, Günter, 23–4, 25, 32, 37
Luxenberg, Christoph, 33, 37

Macdonald, Duncan Black, 97–8, 120, 121–2, 135–6
Macmurray, John, 65, 76
Mahomet et la fin du monde (Casanova), 35
Majesty That Was Islam, The (Watt), 13
Malaysia, 8
Mannan, Khwaja Abdul, 5, 49, 60, 73, 146
Mannheim, Karl, 142
manuscripts, 38, 39, 41–3
Marxism, 21, 141, 142, 144
Massignon, Louis, 98, 121–2, 135–7, 171n1

Matthew, J. G., 61, 73
Mecca, 20, 26
Meccan Trade and the Rise of Islam (Crone), 34
Miaphysite Christianity, 31, 32
Middle East, 8, 150–1
Miles, George, 29
Mishkat al-anwar, 'The Niche of Lights' (al-Ghazali), 120
missionaries, 93–5, 117–21
monotheism, 31, 34–5
Muhammad, Prophet, 10–11, 14, 19
  and Bell, 123–6
  and Carlyle, 91–3, 109–10
  and Christianity, 31, 32–3
  and life, 23, 24–5, 26
  and monotheism, 35
  and Muir, 112–13, 114
  and the Qur'an, 37, 43
  and Scotland, 87–8
  and Watt, 20–2, 140–1, 167
  and women, 148–9
Muhammad at Mecca (Watt), 10, 14, 21, 109, 140, 159, 167
Muhammad at Medina (Watt), 10, 109, 140, 159, 167
Muhammad: Prophet and Statesman (Watt), 10, 11, 159
Muhammadan Controversy, The (Muir), 113–14
Muhammad's Mecca: History in the Qur'an (Watt), 27
Muir, Sir William, 97, 112–14, 161
Al-munqidh min al-dalal (The Deliverer from Error) (al-Ghazali), 11–12
Muslim Intellectual: a Study of al-Ghazali (Watt), 12, 167
Muslim–Christian Encounters: Perceptions and Misperceptions (Watt), 13, 80, 162, 167
Muslims *see* Islam

Nestorian Christianity, 31–2, 79, 80
Neuwirth, Angelika, 42
Nevo, Yehuda, 31–2, 35
Nielsen, Alfred, 64
Nöldeke, Theodor, 123, 125, 126

Noth, Albrecht, 22–3, 25
Noth, Martin, 23
numismatics, 29, 31

Old St Paul's Church, 5, 49–50, 61, 63, 75
Orientalism, 138–40, 157
Origin of Islam in its Christian Environment, The (Bell), 99, 123–4
Ottoman Empire, 90, 96–7, 108, 116–17
Ottoman Poems (Gibb), 96, 116

pacifism, 5, 72
Padwick, Constance, 63, 75, 94
Pakistan, 7, 8
Palestine, 16, 26, 76, 151
Pansebeia, or a View of All the Religions of the World (Ross), 90, 108
papyrology, 29, 44n14
Paterson, Alexander, 93–4
Pfander, Carl, 113
Popp, Volker, 31
'Predestination and Free Will in Islam' (Watt), 5
Pretzl, Otto, 39, 40, 42
Prideaux, Humphrey, 91

Quellenkritische Untersuchungen zu Themen, Formen, und Tendenzen frühislamischer Geschichsüberlieferung (Source-critical Investigations into Themes, Forms, and Agendas of Early Islamic Historical Tradition) (Noth), 22–3
Qur'an, the, 23–5, 33, 36–43, 151–4
  and Bell, 99, 125–7
  and Carlyle, 91–2
  and Germany, 123
  and translation, 89–90, 108
  and Watt, 162, 168
Qur'an – Translated, with a Critical Rearrangement of the Surahs (Bell), 126
Qur'anic Studies (Wansbrough), 24–5

Reality of God, The (Watt), 13, 144
Rebuke of Islam, The (Gairdner), 120
religion *see* Christianity; Islam; Judaism
Religious Attitude and Life in Islam, The (Macdonald), 121
religious pluralism, 78–9, 83
Religious Truth for Our Time (Watt), 14
Reproach of Islam, The (Gairdner), 120
Ritchie, A. D., 76
Robertson, Edward, 98, 122
Robertson Smith, William, 96, 114, 115–16, 117
Ross, Alexander, 89–90, 108–9, 131
Rushdie, Salman, 13

Sacy, Silvestre de, 115
Said, Hakim Mohammed, 172n11
St Mary's, The Boltons, 49, 64, 74–5
Sasanian Empire, 29, 31
Scarborough commission, 128, 129
Schacht, Josef, 22, 25
Schimmel, Annemarie, 8–9
School of Oriental Studies, 62–3
Schwally, Friedrich, 123
science, 85, 101–2, 129
Scot, Michael, 88–9
Scott, Sir Walter, 88
Scottish Parliament, 151
Sebeos, 26
Second World War, 74–5
secularism, 84
sexual pleasure, 84
Sharia law, 148
Sharon, Moshe, 31
Sira (Ibn Ishaq), 23
social sciences, 20, 21
sociology, 142
Spain, 88–9
Spitaler, Anton, 40, 42
Sprenger, Aloys, 112
stemma, 38
Stevenson, William Barron, 98
Stewart, Wesley Henry, 64, 76
Student Christian Movement (SCM), 60–1

Sufism, 121
Syria, 30, 31–2

Talbot-Rice, David, 59
Taylor, A. E., 59–60, 72
technology, 101–2, 129
Temple, William, 72
'Testament of a Search, The' (Watt), 4, 67–86
Toynbee, Arnold, 129
tribal humanism, 20
Trinity, the, 14–15, 82–3, 154–5
Tritton, Arthur, 62, 98, 122
True Nature of Imposture Fully Displayed in the Life of Mahomet, The (Prideaux), 91
Truth in the Religions; a Sociological and Psychological Approach, The (Watt), 6, 111, 144, 162
Turkey, 30, 96–7; *see also* Ottoman Empire

Über den Ur-Koran (On the Original Qur'an) (Lüling), 23–4
Umayyads, 31–2, 36
United States of America (USA), 150
University of Aberdeen, 6
University of Baghdad, 8
University of Edinburgh, 3, 4, 6, 7–8, 9
  and African studies, 100–1, 128–30
  and Arabic studies, 98–100, 107–8
  and Bell, 122–8
  and *Islamic Surveys* series, 12–13, 19
  and Watt, 56–7, 58–62, 65, 71–3, 76–7
University of Toronto, 6
'Uthman, 37

Value of Christianity and Islam, The (Gairdner), 120–1

Wach, Joachim, 142
Walmsley, Alan, 30
Wansbrough, John, 24–5, 37
war, 149–50
Watt, Andrew (father), 48–9, 56, 57–8, 67, 68
Watt, Ann (daughter), 64
Watt, Hugh, 69
Watt, Jean (wife), 5, 6, 12, 51, 60–1, 63–4
Watt, Mary (mother), 56–7, 67, 69, 73
Watt, William Montgomery, 3–9, 15–17, 107–8
  and African studies, 128–31
  and Bell, 126, 127
  and Cambridge, 117
  and Carlyle, 109–11
  and diary, 56–65
  and inaugural lecture, 87–103
  and Islam, 138–45, 146–7, 157–8
  and Islamic origins, 26, 27
  and Massignon, 135–7
  and missionaries, 117–19, 121
  and Muhammad, 20–2
  and obituaries, 159–71
  and the Qur'an, 40, 43
  and religion, 48–51
  and Ross, 108–9
  and scholarship, 9–15, 19–20
  and 'The Testament of a Search', 67–86
Weber, Max, 11, 142
West, the, 84–5, 101–2
Whitcomb, Donald, 30
Winckler, Hugo, 33–4
women, 148–9
World of Late Antiquity, The (Brown), 28
Wright, Timothy, 12
Wright, William, 95–6, 114–15

Yemen, 30, 41

Zayd ibn Haritha, 37

EU representative:
Easy Access System Europe
Mustamäe tee 50, 10621 Tallinn, Estonia
Gpsr.requests@easproject.com

www.ingramcontent.com/pod-product-compliance
Lightning Source LLC
Chambersburg PA
CBHW070358240426
43671CB00013BA/2552